In Praise of *road‹*

I just LOVE your book *road*SIGNS; I came acro[ss it] day, and promptly have been unable to return it, [...] useful—it really does speak to me. Well done for publishing something that is so easy to read, yet so profound. Thank you.

Daniela Yarnold, IC International, Aberdeen, Scotland

I have read some chapters of your book and I love it! It resonates with me and I recognize some of the key messages you shared with us during our workshops. I find it perfect in terms of language used, size, layout, illustrations, price—it's a real gem! Most of all—it's also a workbook within a book where one finds tools and techniques to get around the topic being presented.

Dora Lee, Public Service Commission, Ottawa

Your book…is so cleverly written, I'm really enjoying the read. I find I want to take a section at a time to savor it and savor the intimate look into your thoughts and perspectives.

Christy Moe Marek, restaurateur, Minnesota

I like your book—the size, title, cover page, format and content. I found in it the kind of reminders that are helpful if we have the desire to stay "on course."

Lucy Rinaldi, teacher, Montreal

Betty has a voracious appetite for reading and assimilating the wisdom of current literature. Then she adds her own delightful and insightful perspective. She has created an accessible, rich and multidimensional guide. *road*SIGNS is a gem—a bouquet of thought, interpretation and suggested routes. Thank you!

Julia Cipriani, consultant and trainer, Ottawa

I've been meaning to write you to tell you how much I enjoyed *road*SIGNS. I use it as my morning reading, working with a chapter at a time. I thought it was really well-written and very accessible and I liked your slant on the concepts.

Ron Van Dyke, Regional Sales Manager, ICN Canada, Vancouver

I think Betty Healey's *road*SIGNS is a fantastic book for people seeking ways to slow down and evaluate the direction they're traveling in life. Betty's writing is light, understandable and, most importantly for me and I think many others, approachable. She uses her own life as an example and relates to her readers, rather than separating herself from them. For today's super-busy professionals, I think *road*SIGNS is a valuable and highly accessible and useful guidebook that will help them reach the destinations they most want to experience.

Shonnie Lavender, coach and author, Ashville, North Carolina

I have been reading the book by opening the book "au hazard" and reading the chapter for the day. I read very little in English, but the style is so straightforward that I feel like I could be reading the lessons in French. I am really enjoying the lessons.

Josee Blanchette, Berlex Canada, Montreal

Betty Healey has helped to change travel of all kinds with her book *road*SIGNS. With the use of signs that we perhaps drive by everyday, she encourages us to look at the meaning attached to these signs, in terms of our life. With tips, stories and questions, we can begin to look at paths for our lives that support and challenge us to be who we are meant to be. This is a wonderful little book for self-reflection and for small groups to use when considering choices and group dynamics. With its simplicity, it is a book that speaks to all ages and one that could be invaluable for initiating those difficult conversations with others and with our very selves. With its depth, it challenges us to ask the real questions that are part of living with meaning and purpose. This is a book that needs to be on bedside tables, on office desks, in classrooms and next to the chair where you most like to read. It is a book for the road literally and figuratively, and it is a book that helps us to take notice of the journey when we so often focus on destinations that we never reach.

Deidre Shipton, RN, consultant

*road*SIGNS 2

Travel Tips to Higher Ground

Wendy,
Embrace your light, let it shine, allow others to bask in your luminescence

Betty Healey

Betty Healey

Published by Creative Bound International Inc.
on behalf of Conrod-Jacques Consultants Inc. www.roadSIGNS.ca

ISBN 1-894439-27-9
Printed and bound in Canada

© 2006 Betty J. Healey

Design and production by **Creative Bound International Inc.**
www.creativebound.com 1-800-287-8610
Gail Baird, Managing Editor • Wendy O'Keefe, Creative Director

Cover design and coordinating illustrations by Tracy-Lynn Chisholm
Author photograph by Jacquie Milner

Printing number 10 9 8 7 6 5 4 3 2 1

National Library of Canada Cataloguing in Publication

Healey, Betty J., 1950-
        Roadsigns 2: travel tips to higher ground / Betty J. Healey.

Includes bibliographical references.
ISBN 1-894439-27-9

        1. Self-actualization (Psychology). I. Title.

BF637.C5H42 2006   158.1   C2005-907549-X

Dedicated to
Grace "Connie" Hayes,
my mother and great teacher,
and
Dorothy Healey,
my mother-in-law and cheerleader

A path through the desert is not a detour.
Who did not suffer from emptiness,
cannot handle abundance.
Who never lost the path,
does not appreciate the signpost.

Schwanecke

Acknowledgments

On every step of the journey, there are many people to thank. The following people have been my supporters, my touchstones and even some of my *road*SIGNS.

I am in gratitude for the continuous support of my husband Jim, always a cheerleader and fan, the person who challenges me to stay the course and who supports me every step of the way.

And there are many others:
Ron and Dorothy Healey, also in my cheerleading squad;

Linda Johnson, Deedy Shipton and Julia Cipriani—my spirit friends and learning partners;

Lance Secretan, Gregg Levoy, Kathy Pion and Janine Pajot, who took the time to review the manuscript and provide valuable feedback;

Lorna Foreman—my writing partner, who always listens;

Tracy Lynn Chisholm—my illustrator and a light like no other;

Larry Snow, Nancy Collins and Kerry Messer—my writing practice team, who share their writing challenges and successes;

Gail Baird, Wendy O'Keefe, Lindsay Dods and Pat den Boer—the Creative Bound team who have helped me find my way in the publishing world;

Nathalie Goldberg—the creator of writing practice and teacher par excellence;

Aileen Gibb, Delayne Giardini, Deb Clifford and Dawn Joy—friends on the road to higher ground;

My many clients, workshop participants and colleagues, who shared their stories and continue to teach me the great lessons of life.

Finally, I am in gratitude for Tigh Shee, our home in rural Ontario, where peace is easy to find, where my writer's hand is continuously nurtured and where I can hear the voice of my Higher Power.

Contents

The Road More Traveled

It is a warm evening in mid-July. We have gathered at St. Finnan's Church in Alexandria, Ontario, sitting shoulder to shoulder and row by row in this century-old church, awaiting the appearance of Canadian singer Rita McNeil. The occasion is the 200th anniversary of the arrival of the Scots to Glengarry County—that part of Ontario tucked away in the southeast corner of the province. The concert will be the closing to a three-day celebration of clan gatherings, topped off by a large dose of pipes and kilts and dance and song.

My friend Barry tugs at my sleeve, "Let's move up to the choir loft where it is less crowded." Jim and I vacate our seats and follow him, moving against the incoming flow of bodies, up the narrow, winding staircase, finally settling into four chairs placed at the foot of the great pipe organ. We are alone here, perched high above the audience below with a full view of the church and makeshift stage set up in front of the marble altar. Jim and I move to the railing, and look down on the sea of bobbing heads in animated conversation.

Jim asks, "How many people do you think are here tonight?"

"I believe they've sold out. I heard there were 800 tickets available," I respond.

"Hmmm. That's quite a few people." I nod in agreement. Jim looks at me. "As of this week, that's how many books you've sold—800."

I glance over my left shoulder to see him smiling at me. "Just think, that's how many lives you are influencing with your writing."

My gaze returned to the crowd below. As it is rare to see so many people gathered in my neighborhood, I allowed Jim's remark to settle on me. It was one of those precious moments when I felt both humbled and in awe.

Since writing the first volume of *road*SIGNS: *Travel Tips for Authentic Living,* I have had many such moments. These moments have served as my own SIGNS, those Significant Insightful Gold Nuggets that tell me to continue on this journey, to stay on course, and to continue writing and speaking. It has been a road that has required focus and clarity, for it is easy to become distracted by self-doubt, fear or intersecting highways.

In my experience, paying attention to the SIGNS and consciously choosing the road you wish to travel requires four things. First is *courage*, the willingness to be more present in your life, to look for and respond to the SIGNS as they appear, and to ask, "Who am I?" Next is *authenticity*, declaring your purpose, and asking, "What am I here to do? What is required to manifest my purpose?" and then, modeling this to others. Third is *love*, an unconditional regard for the person you are now, as well as the person you are becoming, coupled with loving what you do, why you do it, and whom you do it with and for. Finally there is *grace*, a willingness to accept yourself as perfect just the way you are, forgiving your blunders along the way, as well as the blunders of others.

*road*SIGNS2: *Travel Tips to Higher Ground* takes you further down the road of self-discovery, along the road already traveled, the *road* referring to the journey of life, and the **SIGNS** being those **Significant Insightful "Gold Nuggets"** informing your **Soul and Spirit**.

It is a journey that is distinctly yours; one where you learn to love yourself; one that is both healing and revealing. It is in the healing that we become a positive influence in the world, radiant, buoyant and attractive. It is a journey of change, understanding that the only sustainable change we can invoke is the change within ourselves, and that when we change, the world around us responds.

Embracing this journey implies honing your SIGN-seeing abilities, paying attention to what is in your peripheral vision, as well as taking the time to reflect on meaning. As you will learn, SIGNS come in many forms. They may be actual *road*SIGNS along local rural routes, conversations you overhear which seem to be meant for your ears, stories told to you by a stranger or on your favorite radio station, a quote or lyrics of a song that registers and won't go away, or a challenge given to you by a friend who puts you on notice. Whatever form SIGNS may take, they are telling you to slow down and pay attention!

*road*SIGNS2: *Travel Tips to Higher Ground* is intended for all who wish to travel on the road of self-discovery, that spiritual path designed to reconnect you with your purpose and passion. It is practical in nature, sharing everyday obstacles that slow us down or pull us off course. The book could not have been written without the lessons taught to me by my many clients and colleagues. I am in gratitude for their willingness to share their stories through me.

In using *road*SIGNS2: *Travel Tips to Higher Ground,* I suggest the following. Pick the book up. Before opening it, ask "what is the burning concern, issue or question preoccupying me at this moment?" Let the book fall open in response. Many readers of my first *road*SIGNS book have used this approach and are always surprised at the results—that the book responds to their needs at that moment.

Welcome to *road*SIGNS2: *Travel Tips to Higher Ground.* May you travel in courage, authenticity, love and grace.

PART 1

Courage

Courage…is the will to make change that starts the process;
it is the will that invests fire into our passion,
fanning the flames in our soul,
so that we become instruments of change.

Lance Secretan, *Inspire!*

Life shrinks or expands in proportion to one's courage.

Anaïs Nin

On the Inside Looking Out

With every experience, you alone are painting your own canvas,
thought by thought, choice by choice.
Oprah Winfrey, *O Magazine*, October 2003

A young woman sits across from me, a well-organized desk the only thing separating us. She is quite beautiful—tall, slim, dark brown hair cut in a shoulder-length flip, deep thoughtful eyes one could get lost in. As she speaks, it is evident that she is both competent and confident in managing the challenges she faces at work, coming into this job with a solid background in sales and management. At age 32, she is where she wants to be in her career.

As we discuss the many challenges on her work agenda, she asks me if she might confide something that is of concern to her. When I explain that our coaching time together is her time, she says, "I know I look confident to the world, and I am rather bold when it comes to making career decisions and tackling challenges, but I don't feel good inside. I feel like a fraud, I don't much like myself, and I often feel that I am simply not good enough."

She continued, "My husband says he can't understand. 'How can anyone with my education and work experience, with my confidence and abilities, not like themselves?' he asks. I can't explain it either. The outside and the inside don't match."

As I listen, her brown eyes well up with the pain she feels deep down in the pit of her stomach. I witness her ongoing struggle to like and love the unique spirit who occupies her body. I am reminded of my younger self, who at the age of 32 felt very much the same way, and of a husband who, like hers, gave me similar feedback. How could I project such confidence while inwardly I despised myself?

The more I observe and listen to others, the greater my understanding of one thing: that self-esteem and self-confidence are very different human characteristics. Self-confidence is what we project to the external world—how those around us experience us. It is our ability to give direction to our careers and make the significant decisions which guide our lives. Self-confidence is founded upon our ability to perform, to be successful in our endeavors and to be masterful. It represents our *doing self*. Success in the external world does not guarantee, however, that we like ourselves or believe in our gifts, talents and strengths, nor is it a guarantee that we fully understand the width and breadth of our accomplishments.

Self-esteem, by contrast, is our inner world, how we think and what we feel about ourselves, our self-image. It represents our *being self*. It is built upon a foundation of self-love and our sense of self-worth. Self-esteem is fed by our own internal self-talk, as well as all the messages given to us by our parents and siblings, teachers and significant role models, friends and colleagues. If we start with a fundamental belief that we are not perfect, or not good enough, messages from others which reinforce this view will take hold. While we can hide what we believe about ourselves from those around us, self-doubt eventually bleeds into the external world.

How do we overcome a floundering sense of self-esteem? There are no easy answers to this question, nor are there any instant fixes. In his book *Teach Only Love*, Gerald Jampolsky says, "We cannot complete ourselves by getting a 'missing piece' from someone else. We are not jigsaw puzzles that need to be put together by another person." The only person who can create an internal environment of love and self-worth is Me, Myself and I. There is no external "Love Advisor," as this chapter's sign suggests, who can do this for us.

There are, however, concrete steps you can take to build a stronger self-image. They require patience with yourself, permission to allow self-love to grow, the courage to change and a commitment to pay attention to everyday moments.

Five Simple Things You Can Do to Enhance Your Self-Esteem

If:-
J am not
tired

1. **Listen** to your self-talk, that tape running in your head. What messages are you feeding yourself? Are they positive or negative? If they are negative, what would you rather be hearing? Direct your energy to positive internal messages. Enumerate the successes you have had each day and the positive ways in which you have affected the lives of others. Feed these to yourself. If the negative self-talk continues, give this voice a personality and a name. When she starts nagging you, flick her off your left shoulder and replace her with your positive angel, and let her do the talking.

2. **Stop** being a self-bully, in other words, mean to yourself. You deserve better. Treat yourself with respect, kindness and high regard. Find one kind thing to do for yourself each day, whether that is a hot bath, a sweet treat, or asking someone to massage your feet. You deserve it.

3. **Start** seeing the goodness in your life. For example, if you want more love, identify where you already have LOVE and express gratitude for this. When you express gratitude it helps you to identify the positive energy in your life and attract more of what you seek to you.

4. **Learn** to accept compliments. Compliments are a great source of feedback and a statement of appreciation by others. Be gracious and allow their praise to wash over you and be absorbed by your spirit. Say "Thank you for telling me that."

5. **Identify** the roots of your lack of self-worth, perhaps a childhood event, the circumstances in which you grew up, being overweight as a child, seeking perfection… The more specific you can be, the more helpful it is. Now ask, how are these memories or experiences serving me now? What would it take for me to heal these "wounds"? The answer often lies in forgiveness of yourself or another. Write down what you want to let go of.

Making the effort and taking the time for ourselves to look inside and listen is the critical first step in building our sense of self-worth and self-esteem. It is a gift only we can give ourselves. Only we can paint our own internal landscape; only *our* brush can change the colors on the canvas.

If you want to feel better about yourself, start by taking small steps each day to recognize how truly special and gifted you are. Commit to this each day, and one day you will arrive, look at yourself in the mirror and see the beautiful and gifted person that you are.

Travelogue

Reflective Questions
- What are the roots of your lack of self-esteem, lack of self-worth?
- What messages did your parents, teachers, friends feed you that you have incorporated as truth?
- What do you know to be true of yourself that you are ignoring?

Good Voice—Bad Voice

I have given the voice in my head that nags me and diminishes me a name and a personality. Her name is Beatrice—a name I truly dislike—and she is "dirt ugly" to match her nagging voice. She sits on my left shoulder and screams in my ear, "You are not good enough!" When I tire of her (and I tolerate her less every day), I flick her off my shoulder and allow myself to tune into Beth, with the soft voice, the one who builds me up and sees only the best in me. She is my angel spirit.

Create an image for yourself of the Good Voice—Bad Voice, the script that runs in your head. Listen to the Bad Voice to hear what it is telling you. Rewrite the script in the Good Voice and fill the sentences with words that make you feel accomplished, worthwhile and beautiful inside and out. To enhance your listening, personify your voices as I have, or find some other creative way of differentiating them. Be a little playful. Allow yourself to laugh at yourself! Whatever you do, change the tapes.

Travel Tip

Life is all about choices. You can choose to travel it in love or fear. If you choose the direction of love, you learn to acknowledge and celebrate who you are, the value you add, and the difference you make in the world. You allow yourself to make mistakes along the way and learn from them, to release the need for perfection. If you choose the direction of fear, you move forward just the same, but are plagued by self-doubt, seeing all that you are not, devaluing your own power and diminishing your importance in the world. The choice is yours—which will it be?

Develop Your "NO-How"

*I live by the truth that **NO** is a complete sentence.*
Ann Lamont, *O Magazine*, October 2003

NO is a word of personal power. NO is a word of courage. NO is a word most of us hesitate to use, for it is firm, clear, a closing. NO means no.

NO makes YES more important, for a sure way to undermine YES, the power of the YES, is to use it too often. NO makes YES special.

NO is about boundaries, knowing when others are overstepping theirs and moving into that place which is reserved only for you.

NO is about discipline—saying NO to yourself when you overindulge, lack focus, or put your personal values on the back burner of your life.

NO is about value, the value you have for who you are and what you contribute, how you choose to use your time and the work you perform.

NO is assertive. It shows your willingness to stand up for who you are and what you believe in. NO is positive, not negative, though it is rarely viewed as such.

NO is an invitation to explore rather than assume; a conversation opener rather than a closer. NO is a life saver and a breath giver, giving you space, a pause between all the YESes in your life.

NO is a verb and a noun. NO is a complete sentence.

• • •

So often I hear, "I cannot say NO to others, I just don't know how. I am afraid of disappointing others, but every time I give in, I end up disappointing myself. What is wrong with me? Why is this so difficult?"

Does this sound familiar? When it comes to saying NO, is it like pulling teeth? Do you feel as though your stomach is about to cave in on itself whenever you utter the word. Is it time to develop your NO-How?

In his new book, *The Answer to How Is Yes,* Peter Block, suggests that "when we cannot say NO, then our YES means nothing. It is a dominant myth in most workplaces that saying NO will be a career-limiting move." Too many YESes, however, may be the straw that breaks the back of our career.

It is also a myth that saying NO will disappoint others; perhaps even have them disapprove of us. We need to disband the myth, embrace NO as an option, learn when to use it and how to say NO with confidence and commitment. Where do we start?

Setting Boundaries

The first step in saying NO is to define our boundaries. So few people I coach have taken the time to consider what their personal boundaries are. Establishing your boundaries begins with your sense of right and wrong, your sense of what is equitable or not, your personal values.

We have all had those moments when we have said YES to a request or demand only to feel that sickness in the pit of our stomach after. It feels like we have been violated. We place blame on the other person for asking, yet the responsibility really lies with us for agreeing. We believe that we say YES to please others, but the effect is to displease and disappoint ourselves. We need to establish a personal code for ourselves that defines what the boundaries are for our YESes and NOs.

An example:

A few years ago, I agreed to work for one of my clients full-time, converting my status as consultant to employee. I should have said NO. Shortly after beginning the job, a number of requests were made of me that infringed on my personal values. I gave in. I should have said NO. Each morning I left the house at 6:15 a.m. to drive the 100-kilometer commute to Montreal, allowing myself ample time to beat the morning rush. I was generally in my office by 7:15 a.m., an hour earlier than most others.

I cherished the morning drive as a quiet time for reflection and planning my day and refused to even turn the radio on. About a month into my new job, my employer asked that I turn my cellphone on as soon as I left the house in the morning as he wanted to have access to this time. I said NO. He pushed, "But I may need to speak with you about something important." I said NO. He insisted. I said, "NO means no."

I learned very quickly that he did not respect my NOs, nor did he respect my boundaries or my need for solitude; and ultimately, he did not respect me. I left the position after nine months, much wiser about the power of NO, much wiser about my intuition and my inner sense of knowing that NO was the right answer in the first place.

We all make mistakes. The question is do we learn from them, integrate the lessons, assume our power and begin to say NO when we know NO is the right answer. Take time to define your boundaries and to understand when NO is the right answer for you.

Decisions are made in your mind,
whereas choices are made in your gut.
Decisions come from the rational,
reasonable weighing of circumstances;
choices come from your essence
and an attunement with your higher self.

Cherie Carter-Scott

Put Your Life Under a Microscope

As you are reading this, you undoubtedly realize that there are aspects of your life where NO was the right answer. Your plate at work is too full; your life is out of balance as you try to juggle family responsibilities with those of your job; you are frequently "bad tired," knowing that too many YESes have led you away from your sense of purpose and your core values. It is time to put your life under a microscope and begin to dissect where you can make some changes, where NO is the right answer. Some things to consider:

- NO is not a career-limiting move. This is one of those myths as described by Peter Block.
- When something *desirable* is added to your plate, decide what falls off. Our plates are not growing larger; they are just filled with more bounty. Know what your limits are and when to say NO. Define what needs to come to an end.

- Clean up your responsibilities and all your "doings." Highlight those aspects of your life that you are truly enjoying. Keep these. Clarify what aspects of your life are nice to do but not necessary. Negotiate these. Consider what you are doing in life simply to please others with no benefit to yourself. These are potential NOs.
- Simplify.

Develop Your NO-How

It starts in your head, without moving your lips. NO.

Then you say it out loud in a small voice only you can hear. NO.

Then you say it louder. NO.

Then you say it to someone else. NO.

You have assessed where you are expending energy in your life, where no benefit can be identified, and you look at yourself and say NO.

You become clear on your work priorities and your current goals. When someone at work approaches you regarding another project, which clearly does not fit in your current priorities, you say NO.

You begin to ask discerning questions in regard to the importance and value of the work being assigned.

You learn to say NO to friends who drain you and YES to friends who nurture you.

You learn to negotiate.

Practice saying NO. Louder! Louder yet!

Copy the "NO U-Turn" sign from the beginning of this chapter. Keep it in front of you as a reminder that too many YESes can derail you.

• • •

The challenge ahead is to change our attitude about NO—to understand that NO is an action word, that it will empower you. NO is not always the right answer, but learning when it is allows you to work toward achieving the balance in your life that most of us seek.

Travelogue

Reflective Question

- What do I want to start saying NO to…at work? at home? to friends? to colleagues? to myself?

Setting Boundaries

A participant in one of my retreats recently turned to me after a discussion about boundaries and said, "I have no boundaries; I have never had them, never wanted them."

"And," I probed, "how is that working for you?" She looked at me for a moment without responding. I could see the "aha" forming. "I just realized it isn't. I have raised four children as a single parent. I have given my life over to this task. And now that all but one has left home, I have nothing left for me."

Having had this realization, we need to be very gentle with ourselves. Many of us have never set boundaries; certainly few of us have ever articulated them. Where do you begin? The following exercise is designed to give you a beginning:

1. What are your core values? What current circumstances or situations are you facing that are inconsistent with these values? What boundaries are necessary to preserve the integrity around your core values?

2. In what circumstances do you experience mastery, that sense of using your learning, personal strengths and gifts, for your work or the greater good? In what circumstances is your mastery overlooked or undervalued? What boundaries are necessary to preserve your sense of personal mastery?

3. What relationships contribute to your sense of wholeness? Who are the 'angels' in your life who support and lovingly challenge you? Who are the people in your life who diminish your sense of personal power through their own needs or by putting you down? What boundaries are necessary to preserve your sense of wholeness?

Core values, personal mastery and personal power are three key areas for us to address when beginning to set boundaries. Unlike the borders between countries, boundaries are rarely black and white; instead, they are a filter for the choices we make everyday. Initiating boundaries in your life is essential if you want to reclaim it and have the life of your choosing.

Throughout this book, other exercises will contribute to your understanding of boundaries. I encourage you to return to the previous exercise regularly.

Travel Tip

Too many YESes in your life will sidetrack you, take you down paths you did not choose for yourself. YESes can distract you from your goals, your priorities or your core values. You need to decide when NO is the **right** answer and have the courage to speak it. Like STP, NO is the additive you can put in your fuel tank that gives you added mileage, keeps your engine healthy and running smoothly, and gives you the space you need to drive the road of your own choosing.

Where Do I Show Up on My Own Priority List?

If we take the time to pay quiet attention,
through meditation, contemplation or reflection,
we may develop a completely different understanding
of why we do the things we do
and a new perspective on how to trust that we've done the best we can.
When we develop the habit of noticing our intentions,
we have a much better compass with which to navigate our lives.
Sharon Salzberg, "The Power of Intention,"
O Magazine, January 2004

Paula and I were discussing the importance of life balance and finding ways to take time for ourselves everyday. I could see she was growing frustrated with me. Finally, she said, "Get a grip, girl! I know I need to take time for me! But the reality is I have no time, my plate is already too full."

Seeing her frustration, I paused. I recognize that my passion about certain topics can be experienced by others as preaching. This was not my intent, so I leaned back in my chair and just looked at her, slowed myself down and tried to assess what was happening. Immediately, I realized that Paula thought that taking time for herself was impossible, another addition to her self-described full plate. Here was another molehill which had turned into a mountain in her mind's eye.

I asked her, "How much time do you think you could give yourself each day?" This is an important question for all of us, for when push comes to shove, we are shoved off our daily priority list in favor of the many other doings that occupy our lives.

Taking time for ourselves each day is something that is easily denied. Our priority list fills up quickly with responsibilities for work, our household, the children and others. When I ask people, "Where do you show up on your own priority list?" the usual response is, "I am not even on my radar screen." When I follow up and ask, "What would it take to get you on the screen?" I am greeted with a look of "you are asking the impossible."

My conversation with Paula emphasized how overwhelmed people are feeling. The search for life balance is illusive. Time for self is simply another thing to add to the daily priority list, a list which is already too full. And yet we all know that caring for ourselves is very important. It's not just about balance; it's about remaining connected to ourselves and staying emotionally, physically and spiritually healthy. We need to create a context, to break this mountain of taking time for ourselves down into a "doable bit." My suggestion is that we start with 10 minutes each day, making the choice to place ourselves as an item on our own daily priority list.

This 10-minute time slot is just enough to pull ourselves out of the fray and to recharge our battery. Ask yourself, "What are the little things that help to ground me, that allow me to have a little space for myself in the midst of my busy schedule?" The following is a short list of practical ideas for finding those precious few moments each day just for YOU.

Carving Time for ME on My Daily Priority List

Linger Longer on the Throne:

Back in the early 1990s, I was the Manager of Rehabilitation for St. Mary's Hospital in Montreal—a busy job with responsibility for eight departments, as well as administrative responsibilities for Geriatrics. I was always in a rush. I had poor habits around nutrition and even rushed my bathroom breaks. As a result, I developed a chronic bladder infection because I never took the time to empty the poor vessel properly. When I realized the cause, the solution was easy: linger longer on the throne. I began to realize that as I did this, not only was my bladder happier, but I was! The seconds stretched to 10 minutes. Take 10 minutes and *linger longer on the throne*.

A Morning Page:

In the summer of 2001, I began a self-study course called "The Artist's Way" by Julia Cameron. One of the first things the reader is introduced to is "morning pages," a technique where you write three pages non-stop each morning in a journal. The technique serves to clear your head and kick-start your day. I now write only one page each morning. One page takes 10 minutes. Try getting up 10 minutes early and giving the first 10 minutes to yourself to *write a morning page*.

The Snooze Button:

I generally set my alarm clock 10 minutes fast. When the alarm goes off, I hit the snooze button, knowing it will sound again in eight to 10 minutes. I give this time over to my spirit and think about the day ahead and what my intentions are. As the alarm rings for the second time, I say a silent prayer, "May everything I touch today be done in LOVE." *Hit the snooze button.*

Driving:

I love CBC Radio in the morning, but I generally postpone my listening for the first 15 minutes of my morning drive. If I have missed my snooze button and morning page because I am in a hurry, I use the solitude of the car, free of voices or music, to kick-start my day. As above, I consider the day ahead and what my intentions are. *Drive in silence.*

The Noon-Hour Saunter:

Whether I am working on the computer or conversing with clients, I need a break about 12:30 p.m. I don't always eat lunch (a bad habit, I admit), but I do like to get away from my desk and go for a walk. I don't need to go far, a simple 10-minute saunter down to the post box and back will do. I often take my work with me, sorting out an issue or generating a new idea as I walk. *Break away and go for a walk.*

The Pet Connection:

I have four cats. Yes, this is excessive—it just happened! When I am feeling out of sorts, anxious or even sad, I pick up one of my feline friends and prop him on my shoulder or sit quietly with Cleo, my female cat, and take the time to connect. Science has demonstrated that pets have a positive affect on us physiologically, reducing our blood pressure, quieting our mood, grounding us in the moment. If you have a pet, *take 10 and make the pet connection.*

Gratitude:

When Jim is home, we take a moment just before dinner to talk about our day, and most importantly, to express gratitude for what the day has provided—good weather, safe driving, a beautiful sunrise, a spirit-full interaction, abundance, and so on. It takes only a moment, but it slows us down, helping us reflect and share with one another. We use that gratitude connection as a dinner blessing. *Share your daily gratitudes with someone.*

To be grateful means you are thankful for and appreciative of
what you have and where you are on your path right now.
Gratitude fills your heart with the joyful feeling of being blessed with many gifts
and allows you to fully appreciate everything that arises on your path.
As you strive to keep your focus on the present moment,
you can express the full wonder of "here."

Cherie Carter-Scott

The seven ideas above take only 10 minutes a day. You only have to choose one of these or develop another practice which is uniquely yours. This is a "doable bit." Whatever your choice, it is a gift you give to yourself each day: time invested in staying healthy and whole so you can be effective in your many other roles. The 10-minute "ME" break is time well invested and is a first step in placing yourself on your own Priority List.

Travelogue

Reflective Questions
- What 10-minute daily practice are you willing to commit to?
- How will you build this into your busy life without creating more stress?

The 10-Minute Spirit Break

Now is your opportunity to make space for you on your own daily list of "doings." Choose one 10-minute spirit break from the list offered on pages 37 to 40, or create your own, and implement this today. Build this into your schedule for the next seven days. At the end of the first week, note how you feel. What challenges did you experience in reserving this time for yourself? Now try it again or something different, again for seven days. Continue until making time for you is as automatic as brushing your teeth. Don't be tempted to give it up. You will be challenged to—this is a fact. Remember that even 10 minutes a day reserved only for you, is an investment in your health and well-being, keeping you fit and ready for the other challenges you face everyday.

Travel Tip

You cannot see the signs crossing your path unless you stop from time to time and release yourself from your busy schedule and the long list of "to do's." Along the journey of life, you need to pull off to the side of the road occasionally and take a break. Ten minutes will do. The downtime refreshes you and allows you to stretch physically, emotionally and spiritually. You create space to take in your surroundings, to see the things which might otherwise pass you by. Don't forget to build 10-minute spirit breaks into your busy schedule. It makes the ride more pleasurable and meaningful.

Cork the Whine and Cut the Jeeze

The soul is dyed the color of its thoughts. Think only on those things
that are in-line with your principles and can bear the light of day.
The content of your character is your choice.
Day by day, what you do is who you become.
Your integrity is your destiny—it is the light that guides your way.
Heraclites

I have decided to have a big party, a real splash! What will we celebrate?
Ourselves. But before we get to this event, I am planning another get-together, one that will clear the air, one that will allow us to see the greatness buried inside of us. Yes, this event will be the "Cork the Whine and Cut the Jeeze" party.

PART 1 • Courage

I have grown tired of listening to myself and others speculate about the "what if's" and "if only's" in our lives. I want to release all the layers of muck that I have allowed myself to accumulate, making me a victim of my own doing, and shift to a place of grace and freedom and living big. I want to grab the brass ring and to ride on the carousel of life wherever it may take me.

With this in mind, I have conjured up an event for unloading everything I believe has ever held me back. You are invited to join me in what I call the Great DUMP! Drive your trailer up to the dumping zone, pull out all the stops and let the "crap flow from your skeptic septic." Don't miss this opportunity to let whatever negative energy you are storing flush down the drain. Yes, you are invited to join me for "bitch and kitsch, a whine and dine, and finally, when all is said and done, the opportunity to dump the "Ah, Jeeze" permanently. It is time for us to uncover our beautiful spirits and give voice to a new song.

This is a potluck meal. You are asked to bring the following:

- salad greens—all those things that through the years made you "green with envy";
- salad dressing—"if only it could have been me" stories;
- crackers—a list of all those who harmed you with their words, the "wise crackers";
- cheese—a list of things that bunged you up and bogged you down;
- a casserole—the mélange of events which, when combined, kept you from living the life you wanted;

- dessert—that list of people you wish would get their "just desserts," the ones who scolded you, told you so, boxed you in, whatever; and, finally
- whine—of course, a good cabernet will do.

Now all of this may seem negative, but this party is the last time in your life that you have the opportunity to judge another person, criticize, complain or in any way feel sorry for yourself. Once we Cork the Whine and Cut the Jeeze, we move on and we begin to see and name all the positive things in our life. We kick up our heels and celebrate all the wonderful aspects of a life lived. We shift from that place of fear to loving and embracing our life as it has been and is becoming; of recognizing, with gratitude, the wondrous life we have experienced, including the lumps and bumps.

You see we can stay in that place of blame. Many people live out their lives as victims. But I don't believe they want to. They simply have not had the opportunities to be heard or to be challenged to move from their victim's world. Each of us can make the choice to move on. Blame, envy and regret act as a ball and chain for our spirit. They keep us tied to the past and unable to see the future.

It is a time for renewal and rebirth. Will you join me? Will you come to my party? Once we have this celebration, dumping the waste we have carried for too long, we can have our Coming Out Party. And that is going to be the biggest bash this neighborhood has ever seen!

Note: All potluck offerings will be cooked and burned to a crisp over an open fire, then buried and returned to the earth where they belong.

Travelogue

Reflective Questions

- What are you planning to bring to the Cork the Whine and Cut the Jeeze party?
- What are the key ingredients? What do they represent?

The Black Dot

1. Take out a piece of blank paper, size 8 inches by 11 inches. In the center of the page, place a large black dot. Put down your paper. Take a moment and look at the page in front of you. What do you see? Describe it.

2. In your description, what did you see? Did you see only the black dot in the center? Be honest with yourself. Did you notice, really notice, all the blank space around the dot? Most of us do not.

If you noticed only the black dot, what is this telling you? The black dot represents all the negative energy in your life—the whines and the jeezes. The white space represents all the wonderful things about your life, the things that fade into the background because of the black dots that seem to dominate. When you compare the two, the white space versus the black dot, you realize that the space around the dot represents a much larger area. So why is it that the black dot still takes up so much room? Like the old 80/20 rule, 20 percent of the issues in our life, those black dots, take up 80 percent of our energy.

When all you can see in your life are the black dots, the things that preoccupy you and consume your energy and spirit, take out the sheet of paper and remind yourself of all the things in your life that you are failing to notice. Choose to let go of the negative and shift to the positive.

Travel Tip

Your bags are packed and you're ready to go, but what exactly have you packed? Just as a trunk full of baggage slows down your progress as you drive, bags laden with troubles and woes weight you down as well. What are you prepared to leave behind: the old story that no longer serves you; those who, in your view, have wronged you; life's embarrassments and foibles? It is time for each of us to lighten the load, to leave the past behind and embrace the now and the future. Once you do, you will take the brakes off your life.

PART 2

Authenticity

Transition…can be a step toward our own
more authentic presence in the world.
That would mean that we come out of a transition
knowing ourselves better and being more willing
to express who we really are,
whenever we choose to do so.
It would mean that we are more often willing to trust
who-we-really-are is all right—is valid and
a person capable of dealing with the world.
William Bridges, *The Way of Transition*

Seeking a Clarity of Purpose

…I actually made a decision that was long overdue.
Sometimes we are forced into directions
we ought to have found by ourselves.
Excerpt from the movie *Maid in Manhattan*

For many of us, knowing the direction we ought to take in life, understanding our true sense of purpose, is not clear. It is rarely apparent to us as the result of a single event. The path is generally not a straight one. It usually zigs and zags from side to side. There are potholes and sometimes sinkholes, places where we fall ear-deep in muck. Most times we do move forward, but there are times when we also retreat.

Clarity comes in increments, layer by layer, like the peeling of an onion, until we get to that sweet center. With each layer there are often tears and struggles, as each of us can attest to in our onion-peeling endeavors.

Clarity comes when we pay attention and allow ourselves to see, hear, reflect and understand, triggering life's great "aha's." Clarity also comes from our association with those important people who are present in our lives.

Finding our way, understanding our purpose, does not have to be a solo act. We attract others to us for a reason; rarely, though, do we call on this energy to serve us in our understanding of self, our path or our purpose. In this chapter, I encourage you to consider the power and possibility of inviting others into your life as guides, mirrors and beacons.

In his book the *Courage to Teach*, Parker Palmer encourages those of us seeking clarity to utilize an old Quaker tradition called a "clearness committee." Palmer describes it as *a time-honored process that invites people to help each other with personal problems while practicing a discipline that protects the sanctity of the soul*. The tradition, however, is larger than coming to terms with personal problems. I use it to seek clarity with major life decisions and for "staying on purpose," calling together my "spirit team," as I refer to them, to keep me in-line and in integrity with my core values and cause. They hold me to a level of consciousness in regard to my intentions. I turn to them when I am struggling with a major decision, a fork in the road, or a question that is consuming me.

An example:

I began my consulting business in 1997. It was always my intention to focus my work on creating workplaces that were healthy for people, and to do this as an independent consultant/coach. How I would achieve this was not always evident. Initially, I worked on contracts in both the public and private sectors as they came to me. I was not clear on who my ideal clients were or exactly what my purpose was. In 2000, I accepted a full-time position with one of my clients, a choice that was contrary to my initial intent. It was an attractive proposal as the VP of Human Potential which seemed, on the surface, to be "right work."

It took very little time for me to realize that working full time for someone else was a backward step on my journey, a major zigzag. In hindsight, I have no regrets, as this backward step led to a significant learning. After a year with the organization, I left, beginning my year-long sabbatical. Making the decision to leave, however, was painful. My pride and ego screamed, "You cannot leave something that you committed to, you cannot stop working."

I hesitated, deliberated and delayed. My spirit team held up the mirror for me, challenging my delay tactics, asking me repeatedly what "I wanted" and how I was called to serve, questioning my fears. It was their questions, their love and their belief in me that gave me the courage to be clear, and ultimately, to move on.

The *4 Spirits for Spirit*, as we now refer to ourselves, continue to serve one another in this way. We all take turns being the "focus person," the person who in that moment is seeking clarity. We avoid offering advice or "how I would do it if I were in your shoes" strategies; no personal anecdotes, problem solving, or being the devil's advocate. Instead, we ask questions designed to help each other to reach a higher level of understanding in regard to our path, our truth. This is the essence of a clearness committee: setting aside quality time to be listened to, asking questions rather than offering advice, mirroring for one another the choices we are making, as well as those we are avoiding.

Sharing our journey, our challenges and our successes with others enhances the quality of this experience called life. We do not need to be alone on our path. I encourage each of you to find, among your friends and family, those people who are willing to serve as your guides and for whom you are willing to serve as well. Engage them in conversations that dig deep and go beyond the casual, that explore meaning and the "big" questions and that help you become clearer. Use the information you gather, the clarity you achieve, to leverage forward movement on your life's journey. Become clear, in the deepest places of your soul, on why you do what you do and why you make the choices you make. This is living a purposeful life.

Travelogue

Create Your Own Clearness Committee

Guidelines for creating a Clearness Committee:

1. Choosing the members of your spirit team or Clearness Committee is a critical decision. Choose those who know you well and who love you unconditionally; who are fearless in telling you the truth and in challenging you; who understand your sense of purpose— your journey.

2. Limit the number of people—usually no more than 4 to 5.

3. When seeking clarity, formalize the event rather than allowing it to be just a casual conversation. Ask your committee members to meet, with you as the focus person, in regard to a specific issue or problem.

4. In advance of the meeting, do your work. Reflect and become clear on what you wish to discuss with your committee. Take time to write about the issue. Write until you have a clear statement of the issue you wish to present to them.

5. The Clearness Committee members are not there to give you advice. There are there to help you become clear on the challenge you are facing and to guide you. Through their questions, you will become clear as to what is in your highest and best interest.

PART 2 • Authenticity

Guidelines for Clearness Committee members:

1. As a Clearness Committee member, your job is to devote undivided attention to the focus person. Quiet the mental chatter in your head. Listen and suspend judgment.

2. The meeting begins by the focus person stating his or her issue or challenge.

3. There is one non-negotiable rule for proceeding as described by Palmer: *Members are forbidden to speak to the focus person in any way except to ask that person an honest, open question.*

4. Questions should be asked in a paced way, allowing adequate time for consideration, reflection and response. Avoid firing 17 questions all at once. Make sure your questions are also well-thought-out and clear.

5. "Why" is generally *not* a good way to begin a question as it is loaded with judgment.

6. Do not give advice or personal examples.

7. If your question does not promote a greater understanding for the focus person, don't ask it.

8. When the committee is over, it is over. This will be evident. Do not prolong the inquiry unnecessarily. Let the focus person indicate when they feel they have enough information to proceed.

Reflective Questions

- Who do you wish to call to your side?
- Who will form your Clearness Committee?
- What is the issue on which you seek clarity?

Travel Tip

It is often tempting, and sometimes even healthy, to travel alone. There are other times when we need the presence of others on our journey. They are there as companions, for conversation, and sometimes just to keep the seat beside you warm. There are special people among your companions who can also be called to serve as guides. These are the friends who love and cherish your spirit and want to see you succeed. They are also the friends who hold you on course by challenging and supporting you. Remember them, seek them out and invite them to join you. They will help you when the journey seems too long, when you go in the wrong direction or when the road ahead is not clear.

Purposeful Choices

…whenever disintegration occurs in life, people have choices.
Some people emerge better for change.
Others recoup the loss and break even, staying the same.
And others spiral downward with despair.
Energy is used in all outcomes, but to create a new set of patterns
or a new structure for yourself requires that you
consciously marshal your energies and give them direction.
Deborah Bloch and Lee Richmond, *SoulWork*

In my first book, *road*SIGNS: *Travel Tips for Authentic Living*, I encouraged readers to clarify their core values, identify their life's purpose and name what they want. In taking these steps, we make the implicit, that which lives in our head, explicit. This is the first step in manifesting a purposeful life. It is, however, only a beginning. We have announced who we are, why we are here and what we wish to achieve along the way. Now the test begins.

New SIGNS, new opportunities, new ideas, new relationships and new challenges begin to appear. NEW crosses our path at every step. The test is, will we stay the course, remain true to ourselves and make purposeful choices. Or, will we be distracted?

Imagine looking through a telescope, your eye on the road ahead. You turn the focus to the right and the image you see through the lens becomes crisp, closer to you, the path forward clear. You turn the focus to the left and the image becomes blurry, visible but foggy, the path forward difficult to see. Each NEW choice we make is like the focus on the telescope: either the choice clarifies and enhances our sense of purpose or it blurs our intentions and pulls us off course. We are asked to pay attention to our choices with each step forward and to wonder if the NEW that crosses our path will enhance or hinder our journey.

Daily, I witness myself and others making choices that distract us from our purpose. The universe challenges our inner resolve to live a purposeful life. The following are some examples:

- We declare we will no longer rescue others. We are prepared to nurture, but state that we will not save others from the lessons they need to learn. Then a new friend appears in our life. Our rescuing instincts kick in when this person begins to struggle with an addictive behavior, financial problems or some other life crisis. We return to the co-dependent behaviors we are trying to kick.

- We declare that our work must be a reflection of our sense of purpose and aligned with our core values. We want work that is integral to the person we know we are and which allows us to apply our knowledge and strengths. Then a new opportunity pokes up its head. It is not really what we want, nor does this work call on our great gifts and talents. The salary and perhaps the benefits are lucrative, so we decide to go for it anyway.

- We declare that we will live a healthy life, filling our bellies with food that nourishes our bodies, and feeding our spirit with positive self-talk and gratitude. Then our mucky mind kicks in, deriding us for something we have not done. We begin to see only that which we do not have and fail to recognize life's abundance. We ignore our intentions, filling our bellies with junk food and our heads with negative messages.

This is our challenge:
- to make purposeful choices;
- to be present in each moment;
- to be aware of the many tests we face everyday;
- to make conscious decisions about how we choose to live our life; and

- to learn to say YES to the NEW that supports our life purpose and to say **NO** to the NEW that does not.

Our life is filled with SIGNS and opportunities for learning on a daily basis. Our success in living this life is linked to what we learn and integrate and how we use this learning for our journey. When we fail to make purposeful choices, we are pulled away from our core values and our sense of purpose; our light fades like a light bulb under a heavy lampshade.

Poor choices, whether these relate to how we live or what relationships we decide to engage in, poke holes in our sense of personal power and, subsequently, our sense of self-esteem. Purposeful choices are the building blocks of personal mastery, that sense we have when all we have learned, all we have accomplished and all we desire converge.

Remember:

Be clear on your Core Values and Purpose

Name what you want

Ask, "How am I called to serve?"

Be mindful of the SIGNS, the NEW

Make Purposeful Choices

Travelogue

Reflective Question

- You find yourself in a situation or relationship where you must make a decision as to how to proceed.

Ask yourself:

How does the decision I am about to make support my core values and my sense of life purpose?

Use your purpose, values and what you want as a filter through which all decisions must pass.

A Daily Meditation

Here is an opportunity for you to place confidence in your Higher Power. Begin each day with the following intention:

Today I will make decisions and form relationships that are in my best interest.
Today I will make decisions and form relationships that are in the best interest of others.

Watch for the NEW in your life. Remember this intention. What would the purposeful choice be? What new boundaries appear?

Travel Tip

The NEW will appear on your journey every day—new companions, new avenues to explore, new places to visit. NEW makes life exciting and the journey more interesting. It is worth pursuing. But before you decide to pursue the NEW, make sure the choices you are about to make serve your life purpose and that they are in your best interest. The NEW may simply be a distraction, challenging you to stay the course.

My Basement Is Flooded

…it is the work of all human beings to attend to
the health of both our "inner" and "outer" houses:
the inner house of our selves, the limitless world within,
and the outer house of the world in which we live our daily lives.
Angeles Arrien, *The Four-Fold Way*

The message on the phone revealed a sense of quiet desperation. "I don't think I can make the workshop, Betty. Here is my *road*SIGN for the day: my basement is flooded. My office, all that is important to me personally, is submerged under two feet of water." The message ended with that. When Josie failed to show up for our day-long retreat, I assumed that she was still battling with the waves that had found their way into her house.

Two days later, we gathered for our *road*SIGNS Book Club. Josie was calmer, sharing with us her distress over what had happened. This same space had been flooded only eight months before, and now, after being recently renovated, was under water again. "What is the message that I am not getting?" Josie asked all of us, wondering aloud about her plight.

As a result of the last flood, she had begun the process of de-cluttering, sorting through boxes of books, purging these as well as journals and other personal items that had accumulated over time. She had just begun this process when the second flood occurred. "I feel so assaulted," she shared. "This space that I created for myself, the one place in the house that I feel is totally mine, a place where I feel safe, is being slowly eroded. For days I have been speechless and emotionless. I guess it is grief. Now I am simply angry and frustrated. Yesterday I began driving through the countryside in search of another place, any place, where my precious belongings and I could be safe. It was irrational, I know, and in the end, it was a fruitless search."

We listened as Josie became more animated. Then her face broke into a smile. "When I finally just allowed myself time, a chance to weep and grieve this loss, I began to realize that the physical space I have created for myself is only temporary anyway. I am beginning to understand that the only permanent sanctuary, the only truly safe place, is found inside me. I know what I need to do: create an inner house that has all the same qualities—a place that is peaceful, loving, safe and calm."

The physical environment, that outer house we create for ourselves, is important. It can nurture or drain us. We feel either safe or at risk. Its features can be energy-sustaining or energy-draining. It is not, however, a substitute for the personal sanctuary we need to develop within ourselves. Likewise, it is not a substitute for the personal work we need to do, that journey of self-discovery.

Focusing on the external house is an easier choice. We can paint walls, buy furniture, choose special objects that inspire us and that bring us to life in their presence. With sufficient resources, it is an easy place to create. But, the walls, and furniture and objects cannot travel with us; they exist only in the physical plane. The more difficult work, as Josie suggested, is the creation of that inner sanctuary. Josie learned this lesson in a most unfortunate way. When she resisted integrating this lesson the first time, it was repeated. The universe created the circumstances to call her to attention and to force her to take notice.

The work of creating our own inner house, where we are safe, loved and nurtured, is work that many of us avoid. Fear lurks in the back corridors of our mind. We believe that we are not good enough to deserve such a wonderful place; we believe that once this place has been built, that we will be too small to reside there. There is fear that we are not deserving of such unconditional love. Occasionally, we are simply not disciplined enough to do the work. This house, however, can only be built by our own hands.

Are you attentive to the SIGNS that are appearing in your life? In what ways are they putting you on notice? Is it time for you to take responsibility for your own journey of self-discovery, to accept the uniqueness of who you are, and to build that inner house for yourself? Remember that, just as Josie learned, each of us needs to create on the inside what we have carved out for ourselves on the outside: a place that is peaceful, safe and calm, a place where love of oneself resides.

Travelogue

Reflective Questions

- What SIGNS are currently showing up in your life that you may be ignoring or avoiding?
- What "aha" is lurking in the corners waiting to be understood?

Creating Your Inner House

Here is an opportunity for you to begin construction on your inner house. Find a quiet spot that will be free of interruptions for a few minutes. Sit upright, both feet on the floor, hands resting in your lap. Close your eyes. Breathe deeply, allowing the air to sink from your chest down into your abdomen. Focus on your breathing. Clear your head of all the personal chatter accumulated during the busyness of your day. Listen to the sounds around you; let them fade away into the distance. Turn your attention to the tip of your nose.

Watch your breath—that sensation of air moving in and out. Hold your focus here for a few moments.

Now turn your attention to the back of your eyelids. You are about to paint an internal landscape—that sacred place where it will always be safe for you, where you are loved unconditionally. Surround yourself with your favorite color; let it linger around you like a warm shawl. It cushions you from pain and fear.

Next, call in LOVE. Celebrate everything you are. Say to yourself, "I am unique. I am LOVE. I am power-full. I contribute special gifts to those whom I serve, to Mother Earth." Repeat this to yourself four times.

Take a few cleansing breaths. Slowly leave the beauty of this place you have created for yourself, knowing you can return here any time you choose. Return to your surroundings, the sounds of your day. Breathe. Open your eyes.

Travel Tip

In your travels you will have many companions, yet there is only one person who will be with you every step of the way: yourself. Develop a kind and gentle relationship with this person, YOU. Love, honor and cherish yourself. Pick up your tools and build your own inner house—that sanctuary that allows you to feel safe, regardless of where you may travel. Remember, the outer houses you occupy are only temporary. Permanence is found within. Your inner house accompanies you every step of the way.

I Believe

I believe for every drop of rain that falls, a flower grows.
And I believe that somewhere in the darkest night a candle glows.
I believe for everyone who goes astray,
Someone will come to show the way.
Yes I believe, oh I believe.

Erwin Drake et al

I believe that big girls don't cry—that emotions are private and should be hidden
away from others.
I believe that life is difficult, a road full of potholes, trials and turmoil.
I believe that the pain of the past should be stored not shared, and that you can't
trust others—family, friends or colleagues—with your truth.

I believe than I am not smart enough or perfect enough or pretty enough.
I believe that when you grow old, you grow weary.

These are the messages I carried with me for many years; the belief systems learned at the feet of my mother and father, from the teachings of "wise" men and women standing at the front of classrooms, from men of the cloth, from family members and peer groups. They do not represent my beliefs today. At a certain point, I understood they were not serving me well. I learned that what I conceive and believe, I will achieve. I learned that my beliefs are a magnet for all of life's other experiences; that negative beliefs mean yielding my power, while positive beliefs mean building my sense of self-esteem and self-worth.

I have been called on repeatedly to re-examine how beliefs can limit and stunt my growth. Today I choose the belief systems that inspire and nourish my spirit; the ones that help me to take flight into my future; the ones I choose for myself. Yet every now and then, there comes a time for a personal check-in—a time to review them again, to *yield to the present moment* and take inventory. I believe…

• • •

Have you ever stopped to listen to the beliefs you have about yourself and how they feed or diminish your sense of self-esteem and self-worth? Have you ever questioned the validity of these beliefs and where they come from? Are they truly yours or did you inherit them from another source?

Our beliefs are like a set of colored glasses. When we look through them, they color the world around us. During my early adult years, I struggled with enormous self-doubt. I was confused about my place in the world, a world I had difficulty connecting with. I felt like an outsider. I was unclear about who I was or where I was going. I was constantly searching for answers, curious yes, but lost as well, hoping that the next job or the next book or the next self-help course would give me the answer…only to discover that the answers were not to be found in those places. They were hidden inside me, buried deep within my memories and belief systems. My colored glasses were shaping my world.

The solution for my confusion and self-doubt was to believe in myself, and in believing in me, learning that I could choose what to believe about myself and my life. I could make choices that turned off the old lyrics stored in the jukebox, and replace these recordings with new self-sustaining beliefs. I learned that it was easy to slip back into the comfort of the old beliefs, the familiar. And I have learned that it takes courage to step into the new beliefs, discipline to stay there, and patience to integrate them. It has been hard work but well worth the effort.

Do you believe in you? Is it time for you to discard the old belief systems that drain you rather than sustain you? Is it time to change the tint of your colored glasses to the color of your choice? Remember, your beliefs harness your power; your beliefs write the script for your future; your beliefs allow you to reveal the greatness within.

We have to discard the past, and
as one builds floor by floor, window by window, and the building rises,
so do we keep shedding—first, broken tiles, then proud doors,
until, from the past, dust falls as if it would crash against the floor,
smoke rises as if it were on fire,
and each new day gleams like an empty plate.

Pablo Neruda

Travelogue

Reflective Questions
- What do you carry as fundamental beliefs about who you are?
- In what ways are these beliefs serving you?
- In what ways are these beliefs limiting you?

I Believe…

Pick up a pen and your journal. Start writing everything that comes into your head in response to "I believe…" Do not edit. Let the words flow from your pen without analyzing the content. Write for 10 minutes without stopping.

Pause. Breathe. Close your eyes for a moment.

Now review what you have written. What surprises you? Is everything you wrote truly your belief or have you adopted it from someone else? Decide which of these beliefs serve you and which do not.

Now write again. Be more thoughtful this time. Write only what you *want* to believe. Once finished, enter these beliefs into the computer and print them. Put them in a place where you will see them frequently—the bathroom mirror, the refrigerator, by your desk. Read them often. Notice the shift in your energy as you integrate these new beliefs and begin to attract to you experiences that support them.

Travel Tip

The belief systems you hold can serve two purposes: they can put the brakes on who you want to be and the life you want to have, or they can accelerate your journey and open you up to new possibilities. It is important to assess whether or not you have your foot on the brake or the gas pedal of your life. You can choose to discard what is not yours to carry, clear the path before you, and embrace those beliefs that nurture your soul and spirit. Then you can enjoy the ride!

PART 3

Love

Love is what we are born with.
Fear is what we have learned here.
The spiritual journey is the relinquishment—or unlearning
—of fear and the acceptance of love back into our hearts.
Love is the essential existential fact.
It is our ultimate reality and our purpose on earth.
To be consciously aware of it, to experience love in ourselves and others,
is the meaning of life.

Marianne Williamson, *Return to Love*

The One I Feed

One evening an old Cherokee told his grandson
about a battle that was going on inside himself.
*He said, "My son, it is between two wolves. One is **evil**: anger, envy,*
sorrow, regret, greed, arrogance, self-pity, guilt, resentment, inferiority,
lies, false pride, superiority and ego...
*The other is **good**: joy, peace, love, hope, serenity, humility, kindness,*
benevolence, empathy, generosity, truth, compassion and faith..."
The grandson thought about it for a minute and then asked his grandfather,
"Which wolf wins?" The old Cherokee simply replied, "The one I feed."

Cherokee Story

Have you ever noticed that you find what you are looking for? More often than
not, I find rocks shaped like hearts, on beaches, on stone pathways, or along the

side of the road. Like rainbows, sunsets, hummingbirds or deer crossing my path, I see heart-shaped rocks as *road*SIGNS, a reminder to be and live *in love*.

Life offers us many choices, but the only choice I believe has any real relevance in the day-to-day, is the choice to live our lives *in fear* or *in love*. As the old Cherokee tells his grandson, we have a choice to make everyday. Do we choose to feed love or fear? The following are some suggestions for feeding love:

Feeding Love to Self

1. *Silence the voice of the self-critic*, that inner voice that wears clothes of fear and diminishes you. I have found that the best strategy is to give her or him a name. I named my self-critic Beatrice. Whenever she begins screaming in my left ear, I silence her with a flick of my finger, sending her flying off my shoulder. I can then tune into the other voice, my love voice, and listen to messages that build my spirit.

2. *Understand the sources of fear*. Where does fear come from? Fear generally has little rational basis. It is predicated upon things we are taught, belief systems handed down to us by our culture, religion or families. Do a little digging and trace back. Identify where your fears were born.

3. *Name the face of fear*. Is it fear of failure or success, fear of abandonment or loss of control, fear of the unknown or rejection? Naming the face of fear builds emotional and spiritual strength. Once it is named, we can understand it, we can shift it to love and engage differently.

4. *The answer is inside of you*. We too often believe that the answers to our problems are found outside ourselves. In *Teach Only Love*, Gerald Jampolsky teaches, "We cannot complete ourselves by getting a missing piece from someone else. We are not jigsaw puzzles that need to be put together by another person." Love resides within us.

5. *Know GOD*. Develop a relationship with your higher power, the universal energy that connects all of us, one to another. Allow this relationship to feed and sustain you when you find yourself in doubt or in the grips of worry. Name your fear and give it up, saying, "in thine hands."

Feeding Love to Others

6. *Be a Love Finder versus a Fault Finder*. Catch judgment before it grips you. Let it go; it does not serve the other person, and it will not serve you. Understand your fear and how the judgment is related. Offer loving energy as an alternative to judgment.

7. *Forgive.* Choosing to forgive serves both the offender and the holder. Forgiveness means correcting the misperception that another person has harmed you; indeed, if you feel harmed, that is your choice. Lack of forgiveness is like a hard knot in your chest. It holds you in the grip of fear. The offender is generally unaware of his offence. Understand that forgiveness does not imply agreement with the action, choices or tactics of another. Let go, release and return to love.

8. *Build bridges*. Too often conflict arises because we have forgotten what we share. Our focus shifts to the differences, all the things that we disagree on and which separate us. Move beyond this. Ask, "What do I share with this person?" Build from this loving place. A focus on differences is built upon fear.

9. *Be a receiver and a giver*. So often I hear people saying, "I know how to give but not to receive. I don't like it when others give me things." Giving and receiving is an exchange of energy and it is an exchange of love. We need a balance of both in our lives to complete the cycle. Learn to be gracious and accept the gifts of love that are offered to you. You will be a much more loving giver and you will honor the gifts others give you.

10. *Express gratitude*. We frequently forget to be thankful, for the gift of others in our lives or for the simple gifts that show up daily in our lives. Build spirit by embracing a practice of gratitude and sharing this with others. We need light bearers on the planet, not shade dwellers.

I frequently find myself imagining a world without fear. It is a big dream, one that can be overwhelming if I am not careful. Then I remember that to create this world requires only one thing, that we love our self. Once we arrive here, we can love others expansively and genuinely. Will you join me on this path?

Travelogue

Reflective Questions
- What is my greatest fear? *Rejection*
- Where does this come from? *Childhood experiances.*
- What does this look like if I shift to love? *Security!!*

Making the Shift From Fear to Love
Like any other shift, fear to love is not an on-off switch; it is more like a dimmer switch where you turn up the light on love, while decreasing the focus on fear. It is a retraining process.

Over the period of one week, examine your choices on a daily basis and take note. Are you a love finder or a fault finder? a love giver or a love seeker? a bridge builder or a bridge breaker? Keep track of your choices; you will see both progress and stumbles. Be steady—keep turning up the light on love.

Travel Tip

A choice to live in fear significantly limits your experience of life, limits the choices you make as you travel, and narrows the road before you. Ask yourself, "Is this how I want to live, to journey? What would open up for me if I shifted from fear to love?" I encourage you to choose LOVE.

The Power of Words

Words are the thunders of the mind.
Words are the refinement of the flesh.
Words are the responses to the thousand
curvaceous moments—we just manage it—
sweet and electric, words flow from the brain
and out the gate of our mouth.
Mary Oliver, *The Leaf and the Cloud*

I am beginning to focus on what people say, to pause and really listen to the words that others use in their everyday language. Like some signs, I am noticing that the words we choose are not always intentional; they frequently fail to express what we really want to communicate. More importantly, our words are more than what they appear to be on the surface. As Charles Handy wrote in his book *The Hungry Spirit,* "our words are the dress of our thoughts."

Have you ever listened to yourself speaking, not your tone of voice or volume, but listened to the actual words that you use? In a recent *Authentically You*™ retreat, Anita, one of the participants, described some of the changes she was currently implementing in her life. As she shared her experience with the others, we listened to her choice of vocabulary. What we heard emphasized the "I must do this, I need to do that, I should do this, I have to…"

When she paused, another participant said, "Anita, I hear what you are saying, but what I don't hear is what you want? In your heart of hearts, what do you want?" Anita looked puzzled. "This is not a trick question," I said. "What Dorothy is reflecting back to you is important. We are listening to you and hear you using the words must, have to, need to or should. I am curious, as the others are, is this what you really want?

Listen to your choice of words and consider this:

Are the decisions you are making

- reactive to your current circumstances?
- related to scarcity (what you don't have)?
- coming from a place of fear?

Or are the decisions you are making

- in your best interest?
- coming from a place of abundance and gratitude?
- in service of your purpose; you being true to yourself?

Anita, of course, is not alone. We all fall into the "must do, should do, have to" trap all the time and fail to use the "I want, I desire, I love" options. We preface action by using I hope to, I wish, I will try…instead of saying I am, I will, or any other action verb in the present tense. Without realizing it, we are diminishing our power. As a result, we delay action or fail to manifest what we want.

Words are very powerful and intimately linked to our emotional and spiritual self. Words reveal your fears, whether these are based on the fear of failure or success, fear of scarcity, fear of love or being loved, fear of abandonment or fear of being viewed as a fraud. Words detail your state of mind and how you feel about yourself, both your self- confidence and self-esteem. Your choice of words provides a framework for how you show up in the world, how you are perceived by others and the energy you attract.

In his book, *Inner Wealth: Putting the Heart and Soul Back Into Work and Life*, Christopher Walker suggests that through words, "human beings have a golden opportunity to grow, to evolve, to become more conscious, to reach higher, to dig deeper, to expand and develop, to discover unthought capacity for work, life and play."

Each of us has an opportunity everyday to examine how we incorporate words into our language and thoughts. Begin to recognize that your words are aligned with intention, with your sense of personal power and with your desire to manifest the life you choose for yourself. Consider the following hierarchy of words:

Evolved Language

Intention	Action
Love to	I am
Choose to	I will
Desire to	I plan to
Want to	I would like to
Need to	I will try to
Have to	I hope to
Got to	I might

Disempowering Language

(adapted from the work of Chris Walker)

The next time you start speaking, also start listening. Start with being clear on what you want, and escape the external influence of the shoulds, musts and have to's. Then begin to ask, beyond what I want, what do I desire from my heart of hearts, what do I choose for me and the life I want to live, and finally, what do I love? Release the "I hope to, I plan to or I will try" and leverage these into I will and I am. The more we incorporate different choices into our language, the more we evolve spiritually and the more closely we become aligned with our purpose.

Travelogue

Reflective Questions

- Listen to your words. What are your favorite expressions?
- What action words do you use in your vocabulary?
- What intention words do you use? (If you don't know, ask others for feedback.)
- Do you like what you are hearing? What will you change?

Listening In

It was my friend Ronaye who first called my attention to my choice of words. She challenged me the first time we had lunch together, asking me if I *hoped* to do this and that or if I *intended* to. Initially, I missed her point. She challenged again, "Hope is an open-ended-word. It implies no commitment. Is it your intention to do what you have said?" "Of course, it is," I retorted. "Then say it like you mean it," she replied.

Following our conversation, I became acutely aware of the words I chose both in conversation and in e-mail. Here is your challenge: start listening in.

As you speak, listen to the words you are choosing. Do you hope, have to or need to…or do you desire to, choose to, love to? Notice the difference in the energy of the words. Do your words energize you or deplete you? Choose carefully.

Before you push the send button, reread e-mails. Is your wording affirmative and intentional or is it responsive and reactive? If you were the recipient of this e-mail, would you be energized or depleted. Choose carefully.

Pay attention to your communications with others over the next week. Reword your e-mails. Change your spoken language. Note how you feel. Observe the responses of others. What is happening?

Travel Tip

Just as your car's engine can be tuned up, so can your vocabulary. Just as you see the evidence of fine tuning in the smooth running of your car, so too will you experience this in the smooth running of your life. As you begin to harness the power of your words, and understand their role in manifesting an authentic life, the course of your life will become more focused. Begin to pay attention today to your language and use your language to give direction to your life.

Don't Take It Personally!

Nothing others do is because of you.
What others say and do is a projection of their own reality, their own dream.
When you are immune to the opinions and actions of others,
you won't be the victim of needless suffering.

Don Miguel Ruiz, *The Four Agreements*

People are beginning to filter into the conference room, slowly seating themselves at the tables. Another *Igniting Team Spirit* workshop is about to begin and I wonder what energy this particular group will have and what issue will come up first. I am frequently surprised. I have an agenda already prepared, even though I prefer to "go with the flow" as a facilitator. Flexibility allows me to meet the participants where they are at and put their priorities before mine.

I notice one of the participants in the far left corner of the room, intensely scrutinizing the screen of her laptop. Her brow is furrowed now, the lines on her face hardened into a frown. I am curious about what she is reading on her computer screen and mildly annoyed that technology is, once again, invading this time dedicated to team learning.

It is time to begin. I pick up my chimes and call the meeting to order. I open with a few welcoming remarks and a summary of the day ahead. A small voice interrupts me from the back corner, just above the still-open laptop.

"On the topic of communication, I want to know how to respond to those really annoying e-mails!" the voice says.

Gee, this wasn't on the agenda, I think, but here it is. "Tell me more," I invited.

"The tone…it's so aggressive. It's the first thing I saw this morning. I am really ticked off…"

I decided to probe. "Tell me, when was the e-mail written?"

"About 10 o'clock last night."

"Why would the e-mail have been sent so late?"

"Well, she probably had a hectic day. Sue has a busy job. We all do e-mails late at night."

"What do you think her state of mind was when she wrote it? How do you feel that time of day?"

"Tired," she replied.

"So, is this e-mail, and the tone of it, really about you, or does it simply reflect the sender's state of mind?"

A pause. She looks at me. "Well, she still shouldn't have sent it."

"I agree, but if you take a moment to look behind the message, have a little empathy for the sender and what her day might have been like, what would change?"

"I would see that the tone is about her fatigue and not aimed at me."

"Exactly. Every time we see these kinds of messages, often sent in haste, we need to ask, is this about me? The answer is generally NO. So, back up and don't take it personally. Glean what you need from the message, see the words, omit the tone, and respond kindly and with understanding. Life is so busy these days; we need to have a bit of compassion for one another. If we get caught up in an emotional response, taking things as a personal slight and becoming angry, we will not be able to be kind or compassionate. We will not feel very positive and may even pass this energy onto others who step into our path because our visibility has been impaired by our annoyance."

This was a great "aha" moment for this group, a great beginning to an important conversation and insight into communication and perception. Whether in conversation, at team meetings or on e-mail, we take almost everything personally. This is especially true for those of us who are feeling types. My message to all of us (I am included here) is *get over it!* We have no idea what has preceded the comments, criticisms or conversations, and no idea as to the context.

Barbara walks into the physician's office, detail bag in hand. She is looking forward to seeing Dr. Bach today, one of her favorite clients. The receptionist shows her into the office. Barb notices that Dr. Bach seems tense, but dismisses this and begins her call. Suddenly, Dr. Bach looks at her and proceeds to tell her off. "She went up one side of me and down the other," Barb tells me. "I was so hurt. We have always had a lot of respect for one another and she is one of my best prescribers." Barb chokes back her tears.

A few weeks later, Barb returned to Dr. Bach's office. She felt a little cautious after the last appointment, but went in and began her call. This time, Dr. Bach was her usual self. She seemed to have no awareness of any issue in the previous meeting. No apologies were offered. Everything was status quo.

In debriefing Barb about this event, I asked her to examine if she had any reason to believe that she had annoyed her client in any way. I asked her to consider what might have preceded her appointment with her client. Barb knows that this physician has a difficult practice. As a dermatologist with an aging clientele, she finds herself too often delivering bad news to her patients. Dr. Bach confided to Barb weeks later, that earlier in the day she had to tell three patients that they had malignant melanoma, a serious form of skin cancer. She was quite distraught. Barb was the unfortunate target.

All of this points to the importance of context. When someone offends us with their comments, we need to ask ourselves a few questions:

- What time of day is it? What meetings might this person have attended prior to our encounter? What situations might they still be dealing with that may be affecting their tone?
- Is what I am hearing in the person's tone about me? (It usually isn't.)
- What questions can I ask to clarify the situation?
- How can I model empathy for the other person?

Whatever you do, don't take it personally. As Don Miguel Ruiz writes, "Personal importance, or taking things personally, is the maximum expression of selfishness because we make the assumption that everything is about 'me'." By taking things personally, you set yourself up to suffer unnecessarily. The assumption that "this is about me" is absorbed like a sponge taking on water and stored in the fabric of your being. Doing this repeatedly eats away at your sense of self-esteem and self-worth, and ultimately, your personal power.

Not taking things personally is difficult. I know. I have spent a lifetime trying not to and I continue to learn. When I dissect situations and ask myself if what has been said or done is about me, I feel relieved. I realize that more is going on than meets the eye. I listen with great attention and try to take away only that which I need to hear. I let the tone and commentary roll off my back. Every now and then, I still feel myself responding, that gnawing in the pit of my stomach returning. Then I back up, survey the scene, ask the questions and move on. I am learning that as I make a habit of doing this, situations become clearer, the visibility improves, and I am more objective and more positive.

So, don't take it personally!

Travelogue

Reflective Questions
- In what circumstances do you find yourself taking things personally?
- Who are the people in your life who most often trigger a response?
- How would this change if you stood back and examined context?

Emotional Triggers

We do not always recognize what our emotional triggers are, those moments during everyday conversations where we do engage and take things personally. Here is an opportunity to begin to dissect and understand your emotional triggers. It is best completed soon after an interaction with another person, when you felt personally attacked or diminished.

Start with the right-hand column of the following table and work to the left. In the first column, record, as best you can, the conversation, the other person's words and your responses. Read through the dialogue once it is recorded. Note what you were feeling and thinking, and record this in the middle column. Finally, review both columns again and note what words or body language triggered an emotional response for you.

Emotional triggers Words, body language	How I felt What I thought	As it happened "The conversation"

Consider context:

As you review the table above, consider

- how you felt before the conversation occurred;
- what the other person might have experienced prior to the conversation;
- the circumstances in which the conversation occurred;
- the language that triggered a response in you;
- your personal history with these words or body language.

Emotional triggers, taking things personally, have many layers to them. The more you can dissect these layers, the greater your understanding will be of your response and whether or not you need to feel personally attacked. By taking the time to understand, you will develop a greater understanding of yourself and others and develop your emotional resilience.

Travel Tip

Taking things personally can take you off course. If you allow the sting of another's tone to hurt you, you diminish your own power. Sometimes it is appropriate to stop, even back up, asking, what am I missing here? Is this really about me? What is the context behind what I am witnessing? Put all the information you gather into a giant sieve and retain only the fine particles that make their way through. Let this feed you. Refuse to be diminished by the comments of others. Don't be derailed, and most importantly, don't take things personally.

Marinated in Media

*Television news programming puts a heavy emphasis on bringing
the bad and the ugly into your home, and in large part, leaving
out the good. It's a constant stream of negativity that invades your
living space and attracts more of the same into your life.*
Wayne Dyer, *The Power of Intention*

My friend Margaret, in celebrating her 50th birthday, declared that she wanted
to pursue a dream she had held for many years, a dream of creating a "good
news" newspaper. "The journalistic content," she explained, "would celebrate
the human spirit, the random acts of kindness performed by one human being
for another, the heroes and the non-heroes who live extraordinary lives, everyday. It would be a celebration of the goodness in the world."

As I heard her speak, noting the passion lighting up her face and the emotion she evoked in her fellow celebrants, I too felt drawn to this compelling idea.

What would it be like to pick up a newspaper or newsmagazine in the evening, read it through, and upon putting it down, feel inspired and lighter in spirit? What difference would it make for each of us if our experience of the media was a sense of being "raised up"?

Media has a powerful influence on our lives. Mine starts most mornings when I listen to CBC Radio, our national public broadcasting station. It is commercial-free, focusing on news, interviews and Canadian culture, but like any other station, the news is explicit and usually filled with a higher percentage of negative messaging than positive. Then there are the daily newspapers, the weekly newsmagazines, the television news, and the all-news stations like CNN, most of which is debriefed around the water cooler or photocopier. "Did you hear about…?"

How often do we pause and evaluate the media that we bury ourselves in everyday. Habitually, we turn on TVs and radios, or pick up the newspaper, without discerning what we are reading or what we are taking in. The content washes over us in waves. We find ourselves swimming in a sea of negativity and fear, feeling fatigued and overwhelmed, and losing our natural swimmer's stroke.

Recently, I have decided to put myself on a strict media diet, dissecting the available choices on the television and radio and in written form, choosing to feed myself only that which is newsworthy and inspiring.

A voice on CBC Radio suggested recently that we are marinated in media. I agree. Take a look at the content. On television, for example, an onslaught of "reality TV" now takes up most of the prime-time programming. It is a decade of the best: the best performer (the Idol shows), the best makeover and model (The Swan), the best competitor (Survivor), the best executive (The Apprentice).

It is an era of radical makeovers where extremes in plastic surgery are extolled as the solution to all our problems. What, I ask, does this do for the hidden self, that emotional, spiritual being inside each of us?

It is a time when there is more violence reported in all media than ever before. Children who are regular television watchers will see more than 12,000 simulated or real acts of violence before the age of 14. Violence is the key ingredient in television entertainment, whether this occurs in regular programming, the news, or seemingly harmless entertainment, such as cartoons. Is it time that we start asking ourselves, "What are we feeding ourselves, what does this constant exposure to competition, fear and violence do to our spirit?

In his book *The Power of Intention*, Dr. Wayne Dyer reminds us that we need to become aware of the energy we surround ourselves with, to know what lowers our energy and what enhances it. He points out that television news programming "is a constant stream that invades our living space and attracts more of the same into our life."

I am not proposing that we withdraw totally from media or that we assume an ostrich-like pose. I am proposing that we limit our intake, that we become more selective about what we choose to read, listen to or watch. Let's begin to recognize that the media is only one point of view and that there are many shades to truth. The heavy emphasis on violence, war, competition and corruption is fear-based media. We absorb this, and we begin to live in fear.

But is this really the world we live in or is it what the media choose to report on? It is human nature, it seems, to be attracted to the dramatic. The reporting is not balanced. Where is the other side, the stories of goodness, kindness, compassion and heroism? How would we feel if we were exposed only to "good news" as Margaret suggested?

Like all of you, I want to be informed as to what is happening in the world, but I do not want to feel constantly overwhelmed. I will continue to read newspapers, sparingly, to watch TV and to listen to my favorite CBC Radio programming; however, I will do so with restraint. Where possible, I am choosing to replace negativity, messages of hopelessness, violence, profanity, competition and disrespect with positivity, messages of hope, peace, love, respect and kindness.

Here are some suggestions for all of us to practice in assessing our media diet:

- Take out the binoculars and observe in detail what you are reading, watching and hearing. What is it you are currently marinating in?
- What triggers the strongest emotional response for you: reading, hearing or seeing? I am very triggered by visual images, so I eliminate these where I can. Try to eliminate or reduce your triggers.

- We all enjoy some television. Check out the options to your conventional choices, for example, PBS, TV Ontario, Discovery, TLC and other similar channels.
- Choose movies and read stories that inspire you.
- Make healthy choices for your children; they are the next generation.

This is an invitation to begin making conscious choices, to be more careful about your media intake, replacing low-energy choices with energy-boosting ones. After all, we become what we see, feel, touch and hear every day.

Travelogue

Reflective Questions
- What story have you recently heard, read or seen that truly inspired you?
- What story have you recently heard, read or seen that tarnished your view of the world?
- How did you feel after each? Which choice is in your best interest everyday?

A Story
Margaret, whom I mentioned earlier in this chapter, has followed her

sense of purpose, creating media that inspires others. She is now hosting a radio show, "Everyday Heroes," a program that celebrates individuals and organizations that work toward making a positive difference in the world. The program's mission is to encourage us all to be a part of the solution. The show airs on CHUO, Ottawa, Ontario, Canada.

Listening in to My Media Diet

Make a decision to track your viewing, listening and reading habits for one week. Note:

1. what headlines attract you and what articles you read;
2. what the leading stories are on the evening news, as well as the programs you decide to watch; and
3. what you are listening to on your favorite radio station.

At the end of the week, review your daily entries. What patterns do you see? If you placed negative versus positive programming on a scale, in which direction would the balance tip?

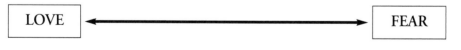

If the balance of your media choices is leaning toward FEAR, try this. The following week, make a concerted effort to shift the balance, changing your media habits to focus on positive programming. When there is none to be found on TV, shut it off, choose some inspiring music and try reading. Search for the good news buried in newspapers, columns such as the *Globe and Mail's* "Facts and Arguments" or "Lives Lived." Read more novels or spiritually based books. At the end of the second week, check in with yourself again. How do you feel? Begin to observe the impact of positive, high-energy media choices compared to negative, low-energy choices in your day-to-day life.

Travel Tip

Every step of the way, you are informed by the news—on radio, newspapers, magazines and television. You want to be informed. You know that living with blinders on narrows your vision, yet you must make choices. Make a choice for the positive. Feed yourself with a daily dose of inspiration. This puts more fuel in your tank and you will be guaranteed better mileage. Be firm in your intention to attract positive and inspiring SIGNS and messages to your life.

PART 4

Grace

To live in a state of grace means
to be fully in tune with your spiritual nature
and a higher power that sustains you....
Grace comes when you understand
that the universe always creates circumstances
that lead every person to his or her own true path,
and that everything happens for a reason as part of a divine plan.
Cherie Carter-Scott, *If Life Is a Game, These Are the Rules*

Off the Hook

If we fall, we don't need self-recrimination or blame or anger—
we need a reawakening of our intention
and a willingness to be whole-hearted once again.
Sharon Salzberg, "The Power of Intention,"
O Magazine, January 2004

We all make mistakes. Mistakes can be our greatest teachers, if we allow them to be. Unfortunately, many of us do not see mistakes as lessons; we see them as just another reason to come down hard on ourselves. We give our self-critic full reign to scream in our left ear and tell us just how stupid, ridiculous and imperfect we are. We are "on the hook."

The scope of mistakes varies from the benign, such as a simple conversation we felt we could have handled better, to the serious, perhaps including issues with our significant relationships, our work or how we are choosing to live our life. The fallout, however, is similar: we don't like ourselves, we put ourselves on notice, we decide to punish ourselves for the dastardly deed. We cannot seem to put the situation behind us and we are out of grace with ourselves.

In the search for more spirit-building and soul-evolving solutions, I have learned that forgiving myself is the key. Likewise, I have learned that the practice of forgiveness is difficult, especially forgiveness of myself. I cannot seem to let myself off the hook easily.

I have come to understand that forgiveness does not mean that I agree with the choices I have made. I am learning to accept that I can make mistakes or have an error in judgment just as I accept that I am responsible for my actions and choices. I have also learned that my gravest mistakes, those instances when I am particularly in judgment of myself, are when I make choices that are out of integrity with my core values and personal code of ethics.

My learning has helped me to understand that I regularly need to connect with my values, my purpose and my intentions, and steer myself back on course. This way, I can change my choices the next time. In forgiving myself for being less than perfect, I open space within me for learning and integration to occur. Then I can move forward with this learning. I grow, I evolve.

The other choice is to not forgive ourselves. This choice ties up our energy; it is a dark spot on our psyche and an emotional burden weighing us down. We have difficulty moving forward. The weight eats away at our sense of personal power, resulting in diminished self-esteem and self-confidence. We become stuck in spiritual and emotional mud.

As humans, we want to be in a state of grace with ourselves, recognizing that we do not need to be perfect in everything we do and that life's hiccups are opportunities for learning. Being in a state of grace requires that we walk ourselves through a process of self-forgiveness, beginning with acknowledging that we have made a mistake or not lived up to our expectations of ourselves. Once acknowledgment takes place, the goal is to learn something rather than begin a process of self-flagellation. It is fair to feel disappointed with ourselves, but it does not serve us to beat ourselves up. What does serve us is to discover what would help us do a better job the next time, acknowledge a mistake as an opportunity to learn, take responsibility and move on, integrating what we have learned in future actions and choices.

Is it time to let your self off the hook? Imagine how much lighter you would feel if you were more forgiving of yourself. Imagine how much more power-full you would feel if you did not poke holes in your self-esteem with barbs of self-criticism. Imagine what else and who else you could forgive, if you were able to forgive yourself first. Forgiveness is not forgetting, it is not even agreement. Forgiveness is a gift we offer ourselves, a gift which releases old baggage, self-judgment, and in the release, invites in new possibilities.

Take time to recognize where in your life you want to forgive yourself. Then offer this gift to others. How does this feel?

Welcome to grace, an understanding that every aspect of our journey, even mistakes, happens for a reason. Grace is also expressing gratitude for all that crosses our path. When we are in a state of grace with ourselves, we can find inner peace. When we find inner peace, we can breathe. When we can breathe, we can finally be totally present in this life and engage in it fully.

Travelogue

Reflective Questions
- Where in my life am I on the hook?
- What situations or circumstances led me to this place?
- What would it take for me to forgive myself (or others)?

Forgiving Self

The following table offers a model for the stages of self-forgiveness. Consider something you are currently struggling with that is preventing you from moving on. At what stage of self-forgiveness are you? What would it take to move to the next stage? Use this table to understand where you get stuck most often.

Stages of Self-Forgiveness

Denial	Downplaying the significance of an event: • nothing really happened • it really doesn't matter • nobody was hurt
Justification	Making excuses for our actions or behaviors: • they made me do it (blame) • everyone does it • the circumstances required it • there was no other choice
Recognition and Ownership	The truth sets in: • I am responsible • I did that? • I allowed it to happen • I made a choice
Anger With Self	Beating oneself up • How could I have been so stupid? • What was I thinking? • I screwed up • I am a bad person
Acceptance and Reflection	It happened, now what? • Let myself off the hook • What can I learn from the situation? • What will I choose to do differently next time?

Forgiveness	I am human: • I make mistakes and that is okay • I did my best, given the circumstances and what I knew at the time • I can't change what happened • I don't agree with the choices I made, but I move on
Moving Forward	Integration: • I apply what I learned to new situations • Enhanced sense of mastery and self-esteem

Travel Tip

Let yourself "off the hook." It is time to flick your self-critic off your left shoulder and listen to a more loving inner dialogue. Give yourself the gift of forgiveness. Forgiveness is the great healer; it clears space for learning and continuing on the journey free of unnecessary baggage. Allowing yourself to forgive, learn and move on, opens you to all the possibilities the road of life has to offer you.

A "Perfect" Ten

As long as you think you can beat the very nature of life itself,
you avoid looking for a way of being in this world
that actually embraces the nature of life itself…which is uncertainty.
You continue to live with the delusion
that there has to be a way to control everything.
Susan Jeffers, *Embracing Uncertainty*

One of my favorite pieces of comfort clothing is a turquoise bomber-style suede jacket emblazoned by a large black number 9 on the back. Because I feel good in it, others generally notice and compliment me on the color and style. As I perform my model's pirouette, they see the 9 on the back and they ask the significance. I chuckle and say, "I'm really a perfect 10, but I hate to brag!"

The sad truth is that for much of my life I have been striving to be that perfect 10, fearful that if I was not, I would be viewed by others as not good enough or as unworthy of receiving their praise or notice.

The desire to be perfect, or to seek perfection around us, is an expression of our need for control—control over our immediate environment, control over the actions and behaviors of others, control over ourselves. We believe, albeit falsely, that if we can control life around us, we will feel good about ourselves, bolstering both our self-esteem and our self-confidence. And it works, temporarily. The house is organized and spotless; we are on top of everything at work; all the ducks in our life are lined up…until something happens to change this state of perfection.

Perfection is an impossible state to sustain, and thus a self-defeating strategy for approaching life. It is a "dead end" that puts the brakes on our ability to live authentically and spontaneously. Trying to live a perfect life imposes on us a set of rigid rules by which we must live. These rules guide our actions and usually influence the lives of those around us. We are rarely satisfied with ourselves or others, because so little in life ends up meeting our standards. In the end, it is difficult to breathe.

Over dinner and a few glasses of wine, several businesswomen bend their heads into the lively dinner conversation. After a busy day, it is good to connect with colleagues and catch up on one another's lives. The dinner conversation is varied, but inevitably turns to matters of the home, for they are also wives and mothers.

I sit among them, a silent observer. I hear the stories of long hours of work and balancing this with family responsibilities. One woman questions the other about all the work she takes home in the evening and she responds that if she did not, she would not meet the expectations of others on her team and her work would not be perfect.

The conversation turns to the home front. An animated dialogue about the correct way to fold and store towels, make the beds and organize the household chores ensues. "I want those bed corners tucked in military style," one of them said, "and I expect my two boys [aged 6 and 9] to have their beds made every morning just like in the army."

As I continue listening, I wonder what the consequences would be for those boys if they failed to comply with this expectation. When did all of these things cease to be important to me? I ask the group, "Why does it matter? Who cares if the closets are in perfect order? What if you worked shorter hours? When is enough, enough?" Shock flowed across their faces, their animated expressions turning to surprise. Is there any other way, they mused? One of them responded, "If we don't set the rules and insist that they are followed, our lives will not be perfect."

My sensitivity to this conversation was that it reflected my former life, living in the grip of perfection. It is a place of fear, fear that appearing less than perfect will lead others to believe that we are not competent or, worse, that we are a fraud. Unfortunately, living in the grip of perfection is a self-limiting strategy, a zone that holds our attention to what *should* be versus what *could* be. The high standards set by our desire for perfection may be attainable but not sustainable. We become disappointed in our performance and find our sense of self-worth being whittled away. We judge the actions and behaviors of others who fail to live up to our standards. In the extreme, we alienate those around us and potentially find ourselves on the road to depression or burnout.

I frequently find myself in coaching conversations regarding PSB, *Perfection Seeking Behaviors.* The following are eight of the strategies for overcoming PSB that have emerged from these conversations:

Strategy #1—Shift From Weaknesses to Strengths

When we are feeling less than perfect, we are seeing only the things we have not accomplished. We are focusing on our weaknesses. Catch yourself, revisit the scene. Ask, what did I achieve? What strengths, experience or wisdom did I bring to each situation in my day?

Strategy #2—See Abundance Before Scarcity

PSB launches us into judgment of others and situations. We see only the negative—what is not being done or the things that are wrong. This is a place of scarcity. We overlook all the positive contributions of others and fail to see what is really happening. When you find yourself slipping into judgment, stop.

Ask, what am I overlooking that contributes to the outcome I desire? What is being done right? See this first.

Strategy #3—Become Conscious of the Unwritten Rules

Learning to let go of our unwritten rules for life is a challenge. Become conscious of what these rules are and what they stipulate. In each situation, ask, what rules am I applying here and why? What am I seeking to control? What is my greatest fear?

Strategy #4—Release the FEAR

FEAR represents False Expectations Appearing Real. Fear is an illusion. Ask yourself, what is the worst thing that can happen? If I do not control this situation, if I release it, what will the outcome be? More often than not, we realize that very little will happen or that the possible consequences are not that significant. Understanding the worst possible consequence is a powerful reality check.

Strategy #5—Know When Enough Is Enough

PSB demands that we go to the limit. We set a goal for ourselves, and then, like the "Energizer Bunny," we go until we stop dead in our tracks. We do not need to do this. Assess your goals and ask, what will it take for me to have a successful outcome? When is enough, enough?

Strategy #6—Start Small

PSB is a difficult habit to break. Go easy on yourself and take one small step at a time. Ask yourself, where in my life is perfection most limiting me? What specifically do I want to address? What do I want to change? What strategy am I going to employ? How will I check my progress? Choose strategies that allow you to succeed—the small things you know you can do. This allows you to build on success.

Strategy #7—Be Gentle With Yourself

When you see yourself relaxing and beginning to breathe again, celebrate. Letting go of PSB is a wonderful thing. Take time to reflect and see what opportunities appear when you are no longer required to follow the unwritten rules. Ask yourself, what was I missing in my life of perfection? What more am I willing to receive?

Strategy #8—Always Do Your Best

In his book the *Four Agreements*, the fourth agreement defined by Don Miguel Ruiz is "always do your best": *Under any circumstances, always do your best, no more and no less. But keep in mind that your best is never going to be the same from one moment to the next.* Our best grows as we learn; it may not be perfect, and that is a good thing for we are learning. When you are tempted to criticize yourself for a performance that in your view was less than perfect, ask, did I do my best, given the circumstances, tools and knowledge I had? What did I learn? How will this change my performance the next time I am faced with a similar problem?

Travelogue

Reflective Questions
- In what aspects of my life am I in the "grip of perfection"?
- How are my Perfection Seeking Behaviors limiting me?
- What am I prepared to do to change?

What's the Worst Thing That Could Happen?

In the following table, list the various aspects of your life where you are seeking perfection. This might include projects at work, your child's behavior, your "perfect" home. Name it, regardless of how simple or complex each issue is.

Under the Why column, record your reasons for wanting perfection in this aspect of your life. Finally, in the third column, record the consequences if perfection is not achieved; that is, answer, "What is the worst thing that could happen?"

Go through your entire list item by item. Focus on the consequences column. How many of the consequences are really serious? How many "perfections" have you named which really don't matter? What are you willing to stop doing as a result of this exercise?

Perfections Sought	Why	Consequences

Travel Tip

Recognize that the life you have, the journey, is already perfect. The "imperfections" you perceive are not what they seem. They are there for a reason. They are the synchronicities that inform you about your path. Trying to control them gives the illusion of keeping you on the straight and narrow, but what is really happening is that you are limiting your own learning and your ability to engage fully in your life. Releasing your need for perfection allows you to "go with the flow," to explore new roads and to enrich this experience called life.

The Body Shop

*To ignite the healing fire, you need to believe something in your heart.
The heart holds the catalyst that causes
the rest of the bodymind to heal in a chain reaction.*
Caroline Myss, *Why People Don't Heal*

In 1997, when I began my own consulting business and assumed responsibility for setting my own direction, I had two primary goals. The first goal was to work with organizations to create workplaces that inspire their employees. The second goal was to work with individuals to help them reconnect with their purpose and passion. To this day, these goals have not changed. I have learned, though, that setting these goals was easy; it is in living them that life becomes more challenging.

One of the *road*SIGNS in my life that has been a reliable compass, is my body. When I choose "True North," traveling in a direction that honors my purpose, my body is very agreeable, free of aches, pains and illness. When I am dishonoring my purpose, my body will also respond, usually in the form of illness or symptoms of dis-ease—an indication that I need to check into the Body Shop and look under the hood. Typically, dis-ease appears when I am not serving my cause or speaking my own truth, when my work is overshadowed by other issues that have pulled me off course, or when I ignore my inner voice, my intuition.

What happens? I am prone to ailments that involve my mouth and throat. In the last few years, I have had six abscessed teeth and all the dental work that accompanies this. During one of my most recent episodes, my friend Ann eyed me and asked, "What are you refusing to chew on? What issue is stuck in your mouth that you need to speak?" Good question, I thought. Friends can be wonderful muses.

The other illness that shows up is laryngitis, usually following a chest cold. Early in the consulting years, I found myself catching one cold after another. This was occurring when a great deal of my energy was focused on work other than my own. I felt I was losing my voice, my authentic power, and indeed, my body was verifying this for me.

Most of us dishonor the vessel that houses our spirit. We abuse it physically with too little rest, poor nutrition and lack of exercise. And we abuse it by disconnecting with our sense of purpose and passion. The emotional and spiritual poverty that results gets stored in our bones, tissues and organs. Take a moment and think about the following:

- In what aspects of your life do you feel spiritually or emotionally impoverished?
- What are the physical manifestations of this dis-ease?
- Where do you derive emotional and spiritual sustenance?
- What steps are you taking to tap into this fuel source?
- In what ways do you honor your body?
- What would you like to change or improve upon?

In her books *Why People Don't Heal* and *Anatomy of the Spirit*, Caroline Myss suggests that investigating our attitudes, beliefs and memories is a crucial step in releasing the negative energy we store in our bodies. Coupled with this is the need to be in tune with our lives as they exist today and the degree to which we are on or off course with our sense of purpose. If we check into the Body Shop, and scan our body systems from stem to stern, we can determine where in our body we are holding stress or pain.

The following table offers you a Body Shop Diagnostic Scan. The scan outlines the seven energy centers of the body, also called Chakras. It provides an example of the symptoms that can appear in that energy center, an affirmation for healing, and a sampling of questions to investigate why certain symptoms are present. It is only a scan, intended to offer you an opportunity to begin investigating any dis-ease you may be experiencing currently.

Body Shop Diagnostic Scan

Energy Center	Symptoms	Affirmation	Investigation Tool
Base of spine	Low back or hip pain Blood problems	I have	What blame am I holding onto? Where in my life do I need to practice forgiveness?
Umbilicus (belly button)	Urinary problems Appendicitis Pelvic/low back pain	I feel	What emotion(s) am I storing or suppressing? What creativity is unexpressed? Are my personal boundaries clear?
Solar plexus	Stomach aches Ulcers Colitis/bowel problems	I can	What is stealing my energy, my personal power? What is my self-critic feeding me? What are my fears?

Energy Center	Symptoms	Affirmation	Investigation Tool
Heart	Pain in chest Difficulty breathing Upper back/ shoulder pain	I love	What emotions am I failing to express? What is breaking my heart? Am I giving more than I allow myself to receive?
Throat	Laryngitis Thyroid problems Dental problems Neck pain	I speak	What truth am I not speaking? What is my authentic self crying out to say? Am I bending to another's will?
Forehead Third eye	Stroke Blindness/deafness Dizziness/seizures Learning disabilities	I see	What am I refusing to look at? What intuition am I avoiding? What personal values or principles are being violated?
Crown of head	Multiple Sclerosis and ALS Multi-system problems	I know	What inner wisdom am I refusing to engage? What is my higher power trying to communicate to me that I am refusing to hear? What is my life purpose?

The body-mind-spirit connection is much more profound than any of us truly appreciate. We feel a pain, we pop a pill. This is our culture. The pain subsides. We feel better, for the moment or until the effect of the medication wears off. Whatever the case, medication is always temporary. Permanent results are affected only when we link physical symptoms to spiritual or emotional causes. I encourage you to visit the Body Shop, to link cause and effect, and to begin to identify more permanent solutions for your physical ailments. Start listening in on your body's attempt to converse with you.

Travelogue

Reflective Questions
- Where in your body do you typically carry stress?
- What are the specific physical manifestations of stress?
- What events or people is this stress linked to?
- What is your body trying to communicate to you?

The Plan From Your Scan

Using the Body Shop Diagnostic Scan offered in this chapter, as well as the reflective questions above, determine which one of the seven energy centers is your storehouse for stress. Highlight this.

Now track back through a usual day for you; what typically are your stressors? Name the activities, work pressures and people that are draining your energy.

Be more thorough. What beliefs are you carrying that no longer serve you? What messages is your self-critic whispering in your ear? Listen in on the conversation.

Make the connection between the emotional-spiritual self and the physical self. What changes are you willing to initiate to address your body's dis-ease?

Make a plan. Write it down. Start with something simple. Keep listening to your body and measure how it responds.

Travel Tip

Every once in a while, you need to check into the Body Shop for servicing. Your aches and pains are slowing you down, you are emotionally sluggish and underperforming. Or, you are spiritually empty, seeing no value in the way you are living your life, having lost sight of what makes you passionate or gives life meaning. STOP. Listen. Look inside your emotional and spiritual engine. What do you see? It's time for a spiritual tune-up, to evaluate what you are carrying with you and what baggage you wish to unload.

Ordinary Time

*Ordinary time is all those days that blend one into the next
without exceptional incident, good or bad;
all those days unmarked by either tragedy or celebration.*

*Ordinary time is the spaces between events,
the parts of a life that do not show up in photo albums or get told in stories.
In real life, this is the bulk of most people's lives.*
Diane Schoemperlen, *Our Lady of the Lost and Found*

In the Catholic liturgical calendar, ordinary time includes all the days of the year that fall outside of Lent, Easter, Advent or Christmas. That means that, according to the Catholic definition, most of our days, weeks and months are simply ordinary.

I find myself resisting the idea that my days are ordinary. They don't feel ordinary. They are filled with extraordinary people, events and synchronicities. My spirit wants to deny any suggestion that I lead an ordinary life. I am making a choice to see the significance of my life and the lives of others. I choose to believe that each of life's little events are extraordinary.

It may be that my refusal to see life as ordinary is based on the times I find myself in. This has been an extraordinary month. I bear witness each day to the emerging beauty of the gardens we have been planting during the past three years and the diversity of colors and scents and plants that are emerging. I watch the hummingbirds that visit our feeders, their "lightness of being" and aeronautic maneuvers, and I think how remarkable these tiny creatures are. I observe the red, grey and black squirrels weave complex paths across the front lawn, burying sunflower seeds throughout the gardens. Later in the summer, I welcome the tall heads of yellow that appear randomly throughout our gardens as a result of their activities. Life in nature is astonishing.

On June 8, 2003, sixty of our friends and family gathered with us here at Tigh Shee, our home in rural Ontario, to celebrate our 30th wedding anniversary. I see my relationship with Jim as "ordinary," what it should be, while others see 30 years as an extraordinary accomplishment. Certainly the event, occurring on a sunny, breezy, sparkling June day, was anything but ordinary. Simply put, it was magic, especially that one moment when the bagpipes began playing "Highland Cathedral" and all of us walked slowly into the garden labyrinth, weaving past each other, greeting and smiling as we made our way to the center. Our ceremony to renew our vows, with our friends Linda and Deedy officiating, followed by the singing of "Amazing Grace" while everyone else joined in, was indeed amazing!

But this was only one day of 30 during this single month. As I begin to pay attention, really pay attention, I am noticing those extraordinary moments in every ordinary day. The more I see, and the more I allow my "seeing" to sink in, the more I am filled with a sense of abundance. Any residual sense of scarcity is waning.

On June 15, Jim and I attended a graduation ceremony at the "Mother House"—a small college that prepares women for work in Montreal's business community. Two of my friends and former students are currently the co-directors of the school, assuming the directorship from the Notre Dame Congregation seven years ago. Their abilities as teachers, mentors and administrators are, in my view, extraordinary. They prepare women, of all ages, to enter the workforce. The employment rate post-graduation for the students is 100 percent. Many of the students struggle to complete the demanding year, some of them having little or no financial resources to do so. Our company provides a bursary for those in financial need and to cover the tuition fee. But completing the year requires more-than-ordinary courage, courage to make a choice to go back to school, to take risks, to take back their power, to study and to succeed.

The month ended with a "working vacation" in Prince Edward Island, that laid-back island of red soil and green fields that flanks the eastern border of Canada. The roadsides were framed by fields of pale pink, fuchsia, lavender, white and purple lupines—ordinary field flowers with breathtaking beauty. An ordinary cab ride home one evening turned into an extraordinary moment when the cab driver decided to serenade us with Celtic tunes from his native Aberdeen. Meals were shared with friends, colleagues and clients—extraordinary evenings of listening, observing and sharing with so many wonderful people living full and eventful lives. We returned home on July 1, Canada Day, crossing four provinces in two days in this wondrous country free of the strife of war and the dangers so many other places experience.

I am learning that as I inhabit my days, call myself into the present moment, I see more of the extraordinary. I am also learning...

- that ordinary days are filled with extraordinary moments when I take time to remember;
- that ordinary people accomplish extraordinary feats when I take time to see them, and know them;
- that behind ordinary faces lie extraordinary gifts, talents and creativity when I take time to engage them;
- that an ordinary butterfly has extraordinary grace when I take time to observe its path from one flower to another;
- that ordinary events have extraordinary moments, great "aha's," synchronicities and meaning when I pay attention.

Do you inhabit your days? Are you seeing all the extraordinary in your ordinary days? So often we feel that life is passing us by. This happens because we are not paying attention. We are entangled in our busyness; life is routine and ordinary. Stop. See. Breathe. Come into this moment. Take a look around you. How many extraordinary things do you see?

Travelogue

Reflective Questions

- Write down all the extraordinary things you witnessed today—in nature, around you at work, what you observed in others, what you accomplished.
- Ask yourself each day over the next month: "Am I seeing all the extraordinary events around me?"

Your Extraordinary Life

One of my favorite news columns appears daily in Toronto's *Globe and Mail* on the last page of Section A. It is called "Lives Lived," and is, each time, an obituary written to pay tribute to a Canadian citizen who has led what appears to be an ordinary life, but who has contributed extraordinary things. I love that someone, a family member or friend, has taken the time to record the wonderful things achieved by another, those same people we see everyday.

Take a moment and write your newspaper column. Write about the extraordinary accomplishments and contributions you have made over a lifetime—your career, your family, a service to your community. This is your opportunity to see the extraordinary in your life.

Travel Tip

Pay attention. Be a sponge and soak up the wonderful events that are happening everyday, the things that you are missing or taking for granted. Seeing the extraordinary in all aspects of your life, those events or synchronicities both large and small, greases the axle, keeps the grit from slowing us down, and makes the ride rich and textured.

PART 5

Work

There is a difference between zestful work
toward a cherished goal and workaholism.
The difference lies less in the hours
than it does in the emotional quality of the hours spent.
Julia Cameron, *The Artist's Way*

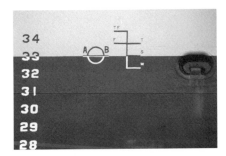

The Plimsoll line, painted on the hull of a ship, indicates the maximum 'loadline' to which a vessel may safely (and legally) be loaded without putting the vessel at risk.
photo by James Howard, London, UK

The Plimsoll Line

I am one with the very Power that created me, and this Power
has given me the power to create my own circumstances.

I rejoice in the knowledge that I have the power
of my own mind to use in any way I choose.

Louise Hay, *You Can Heal Your Life*

You are dancing as fast as you can, while at the same time juggling more balls than you know you can manage effectively—work projects, family matters, community commitments and more. You can't remember the last time you slowed down to a waltz, never mind the last time you stepped off the dance floor. So far you have remained afloat, but you are not sure just how much longer you can. You feel your energy beginning to ebb; your Plimsoll line has been exceeded and you are in danger of going under.

Your Plimsoll line, much like that on the port side of all large ships, is your indicator that you are in overload. Riding low in the water for short periods of time may not put you at risk; you can manage increased responsibilities in spurts. The problem arises when you have to sustain the load over long periods of time with no relief. You become exhausted and overwhelmed, on the edge of burning out. A heavy wind or slightly higher than normal tide will be enough to tip you over, and when it does you ask yourself, "Why didn't I see this coming?"

In my coaching and consulting work with organizations, I have the opportunity to see first-hand what my clients are experiencing. In any given coaching conversation, it is not unusual for me to hear, "It is so busy. I just seem to approach the summit of this mountain of responsibilities when the avalanche hits and I find myself back at the bottom beginning another climb. There is no time to celebrate the little successes or achievements along the way; we just tumble from one project to the next, rarely coming up for air. I can't seem to leave my work at work. It continuously overflows into the other aspects of my life."

The frequency with which I hear this worries me, highlighting my concern regarding the health of the North American workplace as well as the choices individuals make everyday when it comes to work. Take a moment to assess your relationship with your work responsibilities by asking yourself the following:

The Plimsoll Line Checkup

1. Do I feel that I am on top of my work projects?
2. Am I able to complete my work responsibilities within normal working hours?
3. Am I joyfully engaged in what I am doing?
4. Does the work that I do align with my sense of purpose and core values?
5. Do I have good team support and leadership within my workplace?
6. Do I receive feedback that allows me to know that what I do makes a difference?
7. Do I triage my work projects in terms of priority, importance and impact?
8. Do I have a well-developed sense of NO-How, saying NO when this is the right answer?
9. Do I make time in my daily schedule just for me (for exercise or quiet time)?
10. Do I feel "good tired" at the end of the day?

If you are not able to say YES to most of the questions in the Plimsoll Line Checkup, you may be exceeding your "tipping point." Once surpassed, you are in danger of sinking. Rarely is this tipping point predictable, it happens slowly and insidiously. You take on more and more responsibility, attracted to what interests you or what you believe to be your responsibility. "NO" is rarely used in your vocabulary. Without realizing it, the water line is slowly creeping up your bow. At a certain point, the bow dips under the surface and you begin to take on water.

As with ships, the load you assume is affected by the external environment —the culture of the organization you work in, specifically the support systems you have in place at work and at home, the person you report to, the team you work with and the personal meaning you derive from the work that you do. The internal environment, the self, plays an equal role, and includes your capacity to manage multiple responsibilities, your ability to assess your own capabilities and strengths and to know when enough is enough, your ability to say NO, and the degree to which your work aligns with your sense of purpose.

Life is a complex balance between doing and being. Most of you will struggle to find the balance between the demands of work and those of your family and community. Many choices will appear to you along the way; only you can decide what has importance to you and what does not. Only you can decide how you wish to manage the important project of YOU. Only you can develop your NO-How and decide what is in your best interest.

Check in with yourself from time to time to assess the status of your Plimsoll line. Use this newly found awareness to create the work-life balance that you want to embrace. No one else can do it for you. And remember, work is only one aspect of your legacy, the impact you have in the world. Being present as a spouse, friend and parent is equally, if not more, important.

Travelogue

Reflective Questions
- If you could organize your day just as you wanted it to be, what would the balance be between work, time for yourself, and time for others?
- What is the one small step you can take now to shift toward this "perfect" day?

Are You Staying Afloat or Taking on Water?

If you haven't done so already, complete The Plimsoll Line Checkup offered earlier in this chapter. How many of the questions are you able to respond to affirmatively?

If you answered YES to **8-10** of the questions, this indicates you have managed to establish a healthy relationship with your work responsibilities. A score of **5-8** suggests that your work responsibilities are beginning to infringe on other aspects of your life and that your work-life balance equation is beginning to suffer. You aren't sinking yet, but you have been served notice.

A score of less than 5 indicates you are taking on water and that it is critical for you to assess your work commitments. A score of 2 or less indicates "danger" and raises a red flag regarding your long-term survival under the current work responsibilities. Your health may be in jeopardy.

After completing your checkup, assess what steps you can take to improve your score. Make sure that your choices are realistic and attainable. Celebrate each time you take back time for yourself and the other important aspects of your life.

Travel Tip

Check in with yourself from time to time to assess the status of your Plimsoll line, that point on your bow that must remain at or above the waterline so that you do not sink under the weight of life's responsibilities. Use this newly found awareness to create the work-life balance that you want to embrace. When your responsibilities and personal life are in balance, you grow increasingly aware of the meaning of your journey and where your travels are leading you.

Making Mountains Into Molehills

I am only one, but still I am one.
I cannot do everything, but I can do something.
And because I cannot do everything,
I will not refuse to do the something that I can do.
Helen Keller, cited from *Hero*

I have this uncanny knack for seeing the big picture. The problem is that when I see it, the picture sometimes overwhelms me. The idea, the project or the dream is so big I simply don't know where to begin. And the more I think about it, the bigger it grows. Suddenly, what started off as simply an interesting idea, is completely blown out of proportion.

Typically, life shows me the way: a *road*SIGN appears. This past winter has been too long and too cold. We have had more than the usual amount of snow; the snow banks tower above the roadways and country lanes. The wind has been fearsome, sculpting the drifts into waves lapping at the wheels of our cars as we drive by. It is a constantly changing landscape.

Each time it snows, I am outside, shovel in hand, scooping up the white stuff, straining to hike the next shovelful over the banks on either side of the walkway. The molehills have truly grown into mountains this winter.

Every night before I retire, I have the habit of looking outside and down on the snowdrifts below. It is an interesting perspective from this view. What seems so big when I stand beside it, changes dramatically as I look down on it. Their once-daunting size is considerably diminished and much less imposing from this angle. This evening ritual is teaching me that when I change the way I look at things, the things I look at change.

And then I get it: The snow banks are just like all those challenges in my life; when I look at them from a new perspective, they are transformed, and they are smaller and more manageable. It seems to be human nature to make molehills into mountains. We expend great sums of energy over relatively minor issues, blowing them out of proportion, losing time in worry and nail-biting activity. The question is, how do we make mountains into molehills?

• • •

Three summers ago, Jim and took on an ambitious project—creating a garden labyrinth in our backyard. The plan was for a structure 50 feet in diameter, a seven-circuit, crushed-stone path separated by narrow gardens, and a 10-foot center with a water feature. We had collaborators, including a sculptor to create the water feature and friends to help us with some of the initial work. Even with this help, most of the digging and building fell on our shoulders.

We booked a week's vacation for the project. In advance, Jim cut the labyrinth design into the grass. On the first day of the project, I remember standing in the center of this 50-foot pattern and thinking, "How will we ever get this completed in only one week? It is so huge!" I felt completely overwhelmed at the enormity of the task ahead.

I am fortunate to have a spouse who, unlike me, sees the parts before the whole. "Betty," he said, "you do it three feet at a time. Focus on the three feet in front of you. Dig up the grass, till the earth, add the top soil. Then move on to the next three feet. Repeat. Don't look up."

I did as he instructed, and learned for the first time in my life the true meaning of keeping my nose to the grindstone. I kept my head down and my focus on what was immediately in front of me. I did this everyday for five days. Suddenly we were done.

• • •

Building the labyrinth was critical learning for me in terms of breaking the mountains down into molehills, identifying those chewable chunks of doable bits. I have found that the same strategy applies to any project or goal I have that seems to be too imposing or too grand to manage. If I allow them to, the mountains will steal my breath. Achieving them becomes an impossible task; I begin to postpone and procrastinate. But when I take the time to break them down into doable bits, smaller steps that I know I can manage effectively and achieve, I can move forward one step at a time. I begin to experience success along the way as each doable bit is accomplished. I have learned that this sense of accomplishment is what fuels my self-esteem and confidence and keeps me focused.

We all have mountains in our lives. What are yours? Is it time for you to step away from them to gain a new perspective and to ask, what "three-foot" steps can be defined for me to break this mountain down into doable bits? Take the time; it is worth it. Mountains do become molehills when you stand above them. As Mother Theresa said, *If you cannot feed a hundred people, then feed just one.*

The secret in managing mountains is to knock them down to size.

Travelogue

Reflective Question
- What are the mountains that have recently appeared in your life?

Creating Molehills

Sit down with a journal and pen in hand. Before writing, close your eyes, go to a calm place, breathe.

In your journal, name the mountains you are currently experiencing in your life. What are these mountains…any situations that seem overwhelming or too large to conquer?

Now step back and examine the situation from another angle. Stand over it, away from it or just walk around it.

Secondly, discuss the situation with another person, not for the purpose of complaining, but to try to gain a new perspective on it. Have the other person ask you clarifying questions, probe more deeply. What comes up?

Return to your journal and write about some of the insights you have gained from the discussion or by simply stepping away. Can you break the mountain into molehills, those chewable chunks of doable bits?

Make a plan for success. Repeat this exercise any time you feel overwhelmed. It takes only a moment and allows you to shift your view on the issue at hand.

When defining a chewable chunk, remember it needs to be manageable—something you know you can accomplish with relative ease, something that once accomplished will give you a sense of forward movement and accomplishment. These are the roots to your sense of personal mastery and the building blocks of self-esteem.

Travel Tip

The bumps in the road, those challenges that crop up on life's journey, often seem daunting or impossible. Pull off to the side of the road, and look at them from another angle. They will appear different. You will realize they are not really as big as you thought, and you will see new options and opportunities. Break the big bumps into manageable bits. You will gain a new perspective. Then get back on the road and proceed—three feet at a time.

When Did We Stop Speaking?

'High tech, high touch' works best when we use more 'touch'
and learn to use the 'tech' more effectively.
This means taking the trouble to visit with people,
listening to them, and discussing the issues
in a way that includes the personal relationships.
Lance Secretan, *Reclaiming Higher Ground*

As an organizational consultant and coach, I frequently experience buildings that are cold with their silence. I walk through tunnels of "Dilbertesque" cubicles and hear the murmur of lowered voices. I see none of the activity that these offices were originally designed to create, that of a space free of closed-in offices, designed to facilitate communication and enhance teamwork. E-mails and voice mails are the unwritten code of conduct. Face-to-face communication is rare. Meetings to share or brainstorm solutions have disappeared from the daily agenda.

I see employees working diligently, receiving little feedback about their performance. 'Thank you' or congratulatory notes about what they have achieved are unheard of. Celebrations to recognize people or honor their contributions have disappeared.

People hesitate to speak up, to express their opinions, never mind their feelings. When I ask clients why they don't speak up, I am told they are afraid to, or that even if they do, it won't matter; they won't be heard or understood.

Everyday I witness managers and employees speaking in muted shades of truth; people saying one thing and meaning something very different, lacking the courage to voice what is really on their minds. We see the results of this failure to communicate in the breakdown of teamwork, performance issues, high employee turnover, the loss of the joy and fun we once associated with work, and an increasing number of stress-related leaves. We have forgotten that communication is what builds workplace community and spirit. It is the key that keeps all of us connected to what we do and why we do it.

I am painting a picture of the spiritual poverty I see emerging in our modern-day workplace. I wonder, "When did we stop speaking to one another? When did we stop making human connections in the workplace? What will be the road to recovery?"

This is the environment that many of us find ourselves swimming in everyday. The question is, do we want to perpetuate this or do we want to be part of the solution? If work is an essential ingredient in living a purposeful life, are we each willing to step up to the plate and begin to address the growing silence that is invading our workplaces?

The solution to building spirited organizations lies within each one of us. We cannot expect of others what we are not willing to model to ourselves. Where do we start? Here are some suggestions:

Speak up. Start by checking in with yourself. Ask, "Am I so diplomatic in my professional role that I am ineffective? Do I say what I really mean and what needs to be said? What do I fear will happen if I communicate authentically and with candor?" Knowing yourself and facing your fear is the first step in ending the silence.

Meet people face-to-face. We need to engage one another in dialogue. What does this mean? This means looking into people's eyes and seeing the expressions on their face and in their body language. Enough with this distilled communication called e-mail and voice mail. 'Tech' communication eliminates body language, emphasizes tone, and aggravates most of us. People need human contact; choose to close the distance.

Listen, both for the spoken and the unspoken. Remember, words form only 7 percent of any oral communication; the remainder is tone and body language.

Turn off the mental chatter. When you are listening, practice hearing. Too often we hear the first few words and then drop into our own internal conversation. We begin preparing our response to the other person without hearing their complete thought. How frequently do you tune out before the other person is finished speaking? How often do you see others miscommunicating because they are not really listening to one another?

Ask questions. Questions are a critical dialogue tool; one we rarely engage in. Questions allow us to check out our own perception of a situation and to seek understanding. As Stephen Covey suggests, "Seek to understand before being understood."

Clarify before leaping. It is human nature to make assumptions and jump to conclusions. Make sure you understand what the other person means. Paraphrase or ask for more details to ensure a shared understanding of any issue. Suspend judgment.

Tell the truth. There are two ways in which we tarnish the truth: by commission and by omission. Commission means we simply don't tell the truth. We say what we believe others want to hear, or we are blatantly dishonest. Omission means we withhold information. We are not lying, but we are not offering others the necessary details related to a given situation.

Telling the truth does not mean being brutal; it does mean being clear, honest, kind and not beating around the bush. We all appreciate people who are forthright. A lack of truth telling feeds the rumor mill and erodes trust among managers and employees. In the end, this serves no one.

Be kind. This seems to be a lost art form in today's workplace. Find reasons to compliment others on their performance. Tell your colleagues what you see and the difference they make for others. Find ways to support others as well as challenge them in their professional development. Sponsor a "random acts of kindness" week.

Implement "talking stick" initiatives. People benefit from opportunities to gather to hear one another's stories and to be heard. Too frequently, clients tell me they cannot afford to dedicate time for such opportunities. I ask, can you afford not to? Think of it. If we all took the time to communicate upfront, to truly understand differing points of view and reach a shared understanding for moving forward, how much confusion would we avoid in the longer term and how much time would we save?

Bringing people together also builds the workplace culture, offering opportunities for the modeling of organizational values and mission. Celebrating the lives and contributions of individual employees and teams inspires us.

The great challenge facing all of us today is how to infuse the workplace with more spirit. It is a call for each of you to bring the *humanness* back into your workplace, to facilitate the road to recovery for our ailing organizations.

It is time to face your own fears, speak up, listen with the intent of understanding, ask clarifying questions, tell the truth and foster shared understanding among your colleagues. If you do not lead the way by modeling effective communication and dialogue skills, who will?

Travelogue

Reflective Question

- What steps can you implement today at work, to enhance communication among your colleagues?

CARE Packages

CARE is an acronym for Communicate Appreciation and Respect Enthusiastically. Here are some ideas for CARE Packages:

1. Take a look around the office. Who on your team has been working really hard, someone who may be feeling overwhelmed. Or, perhaps it is someone just down the hall who you notice rarely comes up for air. Take them for coffee and tell them how they make a difference to the organization. Talk about your appreciation for who they are and why you respect them. Be enthusiastic and lively in your description.

2. Anonymously send cards to everyone on your team telling them how they make a difference and contribute to the work of the team.

3. Keep a set of inspiring cards at your desk and encourage colleagues to

come in and pull a message for themselves for the day. I use *Heart Cards* or *road*SIGN *Companion Cards*.

4. Try closing your next team meeting with this exercise: Give each member a piece of construction paper and a colored pen. Have each person draw an outline of their hand on the page and sign their name. Have everyone pass their *hand* to the left. Each person marks down the positive attributes they see in that person on their *hand*. Pass again, until all members of the team have added their comments and the *hand* has returned to its owner. Post your *hand* next to your desk as a reminder of the difference you make everyday.

5. Keep rolls of Lifesavers in your desk drawer. Whenever someone goes the extra mile and helps you out, give them a *Lifesaver Award*.

6. Initiate WOW meetings. Ask each person to come with a story about how they "wowed" a customer or colleague. Cheer heartily after each story. Buy small containers of "bubble mix" and blow bubbles during the event.

7. Identify your own unique ways for building spirit at work. Remember always to Communicate Appreciation and Respect Enthusiastically.

Travel Tip

Work is an expression of who you are. How you choose to show up in your workplace influences your experience as well as the experience of others. Face-to-face communication creates a bond among travelers. We are all on the same journey. Take time to meet with others, learn about their journey and speak about yours.

From Tired to Inspired

We are not an airline business; we're in the people business.
Clive Beddoe, CEO, Westjet

It has been close to a decade now since I made a commitment to focus my work on "cultivating values and spirit in the workplace." The journey began with the Continuous Organizational Learning Team at St. Mary's Hospital in Montreal and became the mission of my consulting business. There are days when I believe we—my clients and me—are making progress; and then, there are days that loom like dark clouds on the horizon.

We began the conversation regarding work-life balance in the early 1990s. Organizations decided to introduce a menu of benefits to address the complex lives of employees. At the same time, they made a commitment to tackle the

PART 5 • Work

many issues of the modern workplace. It was a significant positive step in the right direction. One question remains: Has this commitment resulted in the creation of a more inspiring workplace?

In her landmark study, Work-Life Balance in the New Millennium (2001), Professor Linda Duxbury, of Carleton University's Sprott School of Business, reveals that less than 50 percent of Canadians are satisfied with their jobs. Further, commitment to the employer is at an all-time low, and employee turnover and absenteeism is rising.

It seems that the reality of the modern-day workplace models little of the balance we aspired to when the work-life balance initiatives were introduced. Work continues to wear people out, the result of extraordinary expectations, long hours, technology, poor management and leadership, and uninspiring work environments. As a workforce, we are losing interest in our jobs; we are growing tired.

The malaise present in our workforce today is an illness of the human spirit. Many of us have lost that important connection—the secret ingredient that makes us feel that what we do makes a difference to someone or makes a significant contribution to the success of the organization that employs us. We have lost, or are losing, our connection to purpose, and with this, we are losing our way. Many organizations also appear to have lost sight of their role in cultivating spirit and values within the workplace and of creating work environments that nurture the human spirit. This is the challenging reality we are facing today.

So where does that leave us, you and me? What can we do everyday to have a positive impact on the place where we work? In his book, *Reclaiming Higher Ground*, Lance Secretan suggests two critical ways in which each of us can make a difference in creating a more positive workplace: sanctuary and soulspace. Secretan states that sanctuary is "not so much a place as a state of mind…it is an attitude." Sanctuaries are created when groups of individuals sharing common values, such as love, mutual respect and truthfulness, decide to live these values as a code of behavior within their work environment.

Soulspace, by contrast, refers to the physical surroundings we find ourselves in, and the degree to which our work environment is esthetically pleasing—the extent to which the décor and physical space inspire our creativity and engage our spirit.

There are, of course, other essential ingredients for creating inspiring workplaces, but sanctuary and soulspace are two areas where each of us can facilitate the shift from tired to inspired and make a difference every day. Here are 12 spirit-building ideas for you to try:

Sanctuary

1. Encourage your team to take the time to identify the core values that are the driving force behind the team's work. These values should relate to how team members wish to be treated and the team's objectives for customer service and performance.

2. Turn the team's values into a code of daily conduct—a set of standards by which each member of the team chooses to live at work. Check in on these regularly to assess if you are living your talk.

3. Regularly find things to celebrate. Catch others doing things right. Note the extraordinary. Share it.

4. Build community. Choose not to communicate by memo and e-mail. Use your feet. Walk a short distance. Have more face-to-face interactions.

5. Be a coach or a mentor. Support the strengths and abilities of your colleagues and help them find ways of using their knowledge and experience in the work that they do. Challenge one another to stretch and cheer one another on.

6. Make the connection between *what* you do, *why* you do it and *whom* you do it with and for. Help others do the same. This enhances your sense of purpose.

7. If your organization does not encourage flexibility in work habits such as flex time, job sharing or telecommuting, experiment with it yourself and prove that it can work. Build a case for "inspiring" options.

8. As Angeles Arrien suggests in her book *The Four-Fold Way*, live every day the "Four-Fold Way": Show up and choose to be present. Pay attention to what has heart and meaning. Tell truth without blame or judgment. Be open but not attached to outcome.

Soulspace

9. Pay attention to the work environment. Assess what would create a more aesthetically pleasing environment. Decorate your work space in a way that is personally meaningful.

10. Develop a community wall—a place for the sharing of team stories, both successes and great learnings; a place for profiling employees and their interests and lives.

11. Develop the workplace FQ, Fun Quotient. Encourage lunchtime and after-work activities. Build fun into team meetings.

12. Hold an employee "Art Attack" day. Provide canvases, paint and brushes. Frame the results and hang these creations along the corridors and in meeting rooms. Banish barren walls.

Each of us can choose to be an "inspirator," a person who breathes life into their place of work. As Gandhi said, "We must be the change we wish to see in the world." If you wish to be inspired, be inspiring.

Travelogue

Reflective Questions
- Who and what inspires you at work?
- Who and what tires you at work?
- What steps can you take to shift from tired to inspired?

Make Every Interaction Count

Every time someone walks in your office, you have a choice to make: You can grunt, keep your eyes glued to the screen of your computer, and ignore the fact that someone has entered your office (Discount); you can do business only with an attitude of "be brief, be gone, let's get back to work" (Business only); or you can make a human connection by taking a few moments to connect with the person about the work at hand, their contribution to a project, or simply a sincere, "How are you?" (Connection). What will your choice be?

Make a copy of the following table and paste it to your desk. Each time someone walks in your office, make a tick in the appropriate column. At the end of one week, note which column has the greatest number of ticks. Are you building or depleting spirit in your interactions?

DISCOUNT (-)	BUSINESS ONLY (0)	CONNECTION (+)
Your Choice With Every Interaction		

Adapted from *CARE Packages for the Workplace*, Barbara Glanz

Travel Tip

What percentage of your life does work occupy? Most of us spend 50 percent or more of our waking hours engaged in work. Recognizing this, what do you expect from work? A salary, yes, but more than that, most of us want to experience satisfaction, a sense of making a difference, community and teamwork, and a chance to express our sense of purpose. Take time to remind yourself why you work. Stay connected to your purpose through the work you do and the difference you make everyday. This keeps you connected to your higher calling and gives your life and work direction.

PART 6

Legacy

I shall pass through this world but once.
Any good that I can do or any kindness
that I can show to any human being,
let me do it now.
Let me not defer or neglect it,
for I shall not pass this way again.

Mahatma Gandhi

Claiming the Leader Within

Leadership is a process,
an intimate expression of who we are.
It is our being in action.
Our being, our personhood,
says as much about us as a leader
as the act of leading itself.
Kevin Cashman, *Leadership From the Inside Out*

In most arenas of life, whether this is work, politics or within our community, I frequently hear others expressing their concern about the absence of leadership. What is leadership? Most of us equate leadership with power. We define a leader as a person who is in a position of authority, one who has influence over others, as the head of a group, team, department or organization.

The leadership literature would disagree with the above definition, and suggest that what I have described is not leadership but management.

Leadership is not defined by the position we occupy. Instead, it is, as Kevin Cashman suggests in his book *Leadership From the Inside Out*, a process; it is defined by who we are.

It often happens that when I facilitate workshops on leadership, participants want to know two things: who is the best leader in terms of personality preferences and what are the key ingredients for being a successful leader. Participants usually don't like the answers that I give, that leadership is not assigned to a specific set of personality characteristics; that it is the territory of the introvert and the extrovert, the thinker and the feeler, the sensor and the intuitive. It is how we choose to live that makes us a good leader; it is not a specific personality. Leaders may be charismatic, like Martin Luther King, or they may lead by virtue of their presence, like Mother Theresa.

Leadership, unlike management, is not a skill set that we can import from a book or a seminar, a recipe to be learned or worn like a suit of clothes. Becoming a great leader rests on our commitment to do our own personal work. It is an inside-out process of self-discovery, of claiming our place in the world, and making choices everyday to be a positive influence in the world. It is a journey of going within ourselves, naming and claiming our sense of purpose and personal values, and welding these to the way we live. Leadership is a higher calling.

Kouzes and Posner in their book *Encouraging the Heart*, state that "Leadership is not about a position or a place. It's an attitude and a sense of responsibility for making a difference." Leadership focuses on people rather than task; it is invested in the success of others versus personal success. Leadership coaches and asks, rather than controls and tells. Leadership is directed by the heart and the head, rather than by the head only. It is about creating environments, at home and at work, that nurture and inspire the spirits of others.

Some of you are reading this and wondering, am I a leader? Yes you are; the question is, "to what extent do you want to claim the leader that lives within you?" You have a choice everyday as to how you show up in the world, whether this be at home with your family or in the workplace with your colleagues.

Consider this: a clear pool of water, its surface unblemished, smooth as a mirror. You are a drop falling from above, about to hit the polished surface of the water. As you do, what happens? Your contact with the surface sends out a series of ripples, concentric circles. You are energy and you create an energy field around you. What will that energy be?

To be effective as a leader, the first step is being clear on the following:

- What type of impact do you want to have on the environment and the people who surround you?
- How do you wish to be received and perceived by others?

- What is the legacy you are choosing to leave behind?
- What values are central to your leadership?
- How do others witness these values in you?

When you embrace the leader within you, who do you become? By my definition, leaders are:

- generous of spirit;
- a positive influence in the world;
- understanding, compassionate and caring;
- able to heal themselves and support this in others;
- committed to personal growth and self-discovery;
- collaborative;
- self-aware and aware of the world around them;
- of service to others, their community, Mother Earth, a cause;
- committed to their personal values and sense of purpose.

This is an invitation to YOU to claim the leader that lives within you, if you have not already done so. This is an invitation to see the leader that exists in others and to invite them out to play in the sandbox of life.

Travelogue

Reflective Questions

- If you were to describe someone who in your view is a great leader, what would you say about them?
- In what ways do you model these same characteristics to others in your life?

A Leadership Story

Ron would not consider himself a leader. As he humbly accepted an award recently for Senior Citizen Volunteer of the Year, he thanked the person who nominated him and all those in his circle who share the work he does for the community.

Born in central Newfoundland, Ron had little access to education or personal development. He was expected to be self-sufficient at an early age and left school after completing grade four. At 19, he traveled to Cornwall, Ontario. There he met his future wife, and after a brief return to Newfoundland, settled in Cornwall with his bride, Dorothy. They subsequently had six children. With little education but a willingness to work hard, Ron often had two to three jobs. Eventually, he became a millwright at a local factory. After 35 years, he was involuntarily retired when the plant closed. He was 59. He never looked back and began his second career, pursuing personal interests and volunteering through his church and local community.

If you ask Ron about leadership, he'll just grin and say, "Ah, that's for them other fellas. I always refused those management jobs at work. I didn't want to have to boss people around." Like many others, he equates leadership with management. But to us, his children and grandchildren, friends and colleagues, Ron is a leader. When he was younger, he was a Boy Scout leader, hockey coach and referee, and was, for a time, head of the hockey referees for the Cornwall district. With Dorothy, he taught marriage-preparation courses. Today, he works for the St. Vincent de Paul Food Bank, tirelessly raising money and seeking donations to feed the less fortunate. He visits shut-ins and takes others to doctor's and hospital appointments. Neighbors know to call him if they are in need of a helping hand. He is a well-known presence and community leader.

Ron deserved that award he was given on Canada Day 2004. At the age of 75, he is tireless, a positive role model. Ron is my father-in-law and I am eternally grateful to have him in my life.

Now…

Write a story about one of your leader-heroes. Don't forget to send them a copy of the story or to thank and support them. Then, remember their story everyday and ask yourself, what will my story be?

Travel Tip

Your experience of the journey of life is an expression of how you choose to lead. It is an awareness of how you influence the world around you and the people who cross your path everyday. Choose to live large. Be generous with yourself and with others. Have an impact on every road you travel by being a positive influence. Change the world you live in by being authentically you, true to your purpose and your passion.

Put on Notice

I will not die an unlived life.
I will not live in fear of falling or catching fire.
I choose to inhabit my days, to allow my living to open me,
to make me less afraid, more accessible;
to loosen my heart until it becomes a wing, a torch, a promise.
I choose to risk my significance, to live so that which
came to me as seed, goes to the next as blossom, and that
which came to me as blossom, goes on as fruit.
Dawna Markova, *I Will Not Die an Unlived Life*

As so often happens, every now and then life puts us on notice. The large hand of the universe wraps itself tightly around your chest, squeezing hard, so hard you feel as though your chest is being crushed. Midway through the writing of this book, my friend, creative collaborator and kindred spirit Tracy-Lynn called me.

"I have very sad news," she began, "my sister Julie was in a very bad car accident early yesterday morning. She didn't make it. She's gone."

My immediate response was shock and denial, "That's not possible, Tracy; we were just talking about her the other day and her plans to become a nutritionist, her natural talent for understanding others, her…"

Tracy is very rational and clear, "She's gone. She didn't suffer. She had a really bad head injury, it's better this way."

I found myself weeping, feeling my heart breaking, choking out the words, "I'm so sorry, Tracy."

It is in these moments that those who have suffered the greatest loss are there to comfort us. "It's okay, Betty, it's okay," Tracy says.

Since then, I have found myself in tears many times, weeping for the loss of this young, vital spirit in the budding days of her life, so much of her potential not yet witnessed by the world. I have wept for Tracy, for her parents, and for all her friends who were so vitally linked to her. And I wept for all of us who take life for granted, who walk through our days without really inhabiting them. As is the way, it is only when life puts us on notice, that we really pay attention.

I shared my sadness with members of the *road*SIGNS Book Club. Our conversation turned to this question, "What does it mean to fully inhabit our days, to be truly present? What would change if we saw the many SIGNS in our life and chose to live by the messages they offer us?" This is not a question to which we can find an easy answer.

Two years ago, I was given a book by Stephen Levine entitled *One Year to Live: How to Live This Year As If It Were Your Last*. I mentioned this to the other members, wondering aloud how my life would change if I knew I had only one year to live; how this would influence every choice I made from how I spend my time, to what I chose to do with each moment, and with whom I spent time. What is left to complete that is still undone? The idea may seem a little fatalistic, but consider this: How much of your time, how many of your days, stand for something truly important to you, or to others in your life? How many of your days are lost to busyness and unintentional activity?

The death of someone close, especially when sudden and unexpected, sends out a shock wave. We respond. We are reminded of our own mortality. The incident puts us on notice, causes us to stand back and to take a personal inventory. The notice may appear in other forms, perhaps the loss of a relationship, an illness or an unanticipated change. The effect is the same. Life is demanding that we pay attention.

I find myself asking why I need to be shocked into this awareness, why I need to be put on notice before coming to a full stop, questioning why I must "crash" before looking at my life and how I am investing my time. Our habit is to become complacent about life, taking the precious moments for granted, waking up one day and wondering, where did the time go?

The more mindful we are, the less there is to crowd us in our deathbed.
When we are living our life instead of only thinking about it,
nothing remains undone,
and if we should die that day, we are pleased.
When everything is brought up to date,
and the heart turned toward itself,
it is a good day to die.

Stephen Levine

This is my intention for each of us:

May the memory of Julie Bedard and the many friends and family members who have crossed over before us serve to remind us to live each moment more fully and to inhabit every moment of every day.

May each of us refuse to die with a life unlived.

May each of us choose intention over complacence.

And when our time comes, may we look back over our life and say loudly and boldly, "I lived my life well!"

Travelogue

Reflective Questions

- What significant event has recently put you on notice?

- What is the lesson begging to be learned?
- In what ways are you responding?

We Melted in Her Presence

The following is an excerpt from the eulogy given to honor Julie Bedard. The message was delivered by her sister Tracy, but is spoken in Julie's voice.

We are all living on borrowed time. The time you have been given is a gift. The people in your life are more precious than any riches. I want to share with you what I know about living:

- *Don't ever miss a party because you never know what wonderful people you will meet.*
- *Go out and play—always remember to play!*
- *Live with a passion, fiery passion. It will save your soul some day.*
- *Smile at everyone you see, even if they don't smile back.*
- *Bake, bake, bake for the ones you love, and please, package your baking in pretty wrapping.*
- *Travel, explore and be merry. There is more to this world right outside your door.*
- *Always have a bottle of red Merlot handy, because you never know when a friend will come to the door.*
- *Shop until you drop, a girl can never be caught in last year's fashions, and*

when you are feeling blue, just go buy another pair of shoes.

- *Open your mind to the possibilities. Open your heart to all you meet.*
- *Be open to your dreams, bring them to reality. Your life was meant for something bigger than you may be able to see.*
- *Simple riches are at hand, stop and look around. There is magic in the air; there is fairy dust everywhere.*
- *Cherish all that you have.*
- *Never leave without a kiss, without an "I love you" and "I'll see you later."*

So I ask each of you now:

What are you going to do with the time you have been given?

Don't waste a moment. Don't live with regrets. This world is such a beautiful and magical place. Let your light shine with reckless abandon.

I say, "carpe diem." I seized the days and I relished the nights, and I loved and lived every moment of my life. So to all of you I say, "I love you all, see you on the flip side and remember, LIVE. Don't walk through life; dance and sing as I did."

Julie

Travel Tip

When you see the Reduce Speed sign up ahead, don't ignore it. Slow down or come to a full stop. Typically, we glide through, rarely slowing down, not really noticing the landscape around us, not really conscious of the many choices we are making. Time passes by unnoticed. Make a decision to start respecting the signs in your life. Take your foot off the gas pedal, look around and enjoy the scenery, and live your days mindfully.

Crowdy Head
Thanks to Cathy Mauk in Australia

On Being "Joy Full"

The only difference between an extraordinary life and an ordinary life
is the extraordinary pleasures you find in ordinary things.
Veronique Vienne, cited in *Romancing the Ordinary,*
Sarah Ban Breathnach

Joy: a condition or feeling of high pleasure or delight, happiness or gladness; the expression or manifestation of such feeling; a source or object of pleasure or satisfaction.

Houghton Mifflin Canadian Dictionary

PART 6 • Legacy

I am fortunate to attract wonderful and interesting people into my life—friends and colleagues who daily challenge my thinking and the way I choose to experience everyday life. My friend and writing partner Kerry is one of these folks. In a recent conversation she challenged me, "Where in your life do you experience joy? What makes you feel joyful?"

It was not one of those questions that demanded an immediate answer; it was a question to travel with, to sit with and to wear. It was a question intended to create some space in my "crowdy head," pushing over the busyness of the day-to-day. It was a call for me to sit up and take notice of the wonderful things that fill my days and evenings, the things I often forget to take notice of.

It seems to me that joy is a lot like abundance; it is present all the time, but we rarely acknowledge it, and because we don't acknowledge it, we simply don't see it. We slide into that state of complacency, taking for granted the beauty that surrounds us, or we allow the more negative in our life to crowd out the positive. We fail to "en-joy," to infuse our lives with pleasure, satisfaction and beauty.

Being joyful is a choice. How many times have you said or heard another say, "I just want to be happy. I want to have fun, to experience joy in my life." The first step in experiencing joy is to see where it already exists, and as the Law of Attraction states, when we see and acknowledge it, we will attract more of it to our lives.

Following my conversation with Kerry, I took a closer look at my own life and where joy co-exists with me everyday. The following is the list that came to me soon after our conversation:

What makes me joyful?

- Four cats brushing around my feet shortly after these same feet hit the floor first thing in the morning;
- The sound of a gentle summer rain falling in the trees beyond my bedroom window;
- Sunsets and sunrises filled with orange, fuchsia, peach and plum;
- The first tulips poking through the earth on an early spring day;
- Working in my garden and seeing the results of my loving hands come to bloom;
- The "aha" moments I see on my clients faces when they "get it";
- Watching people open up to themselves and one another in the safety of a retreat environment;
- Receiving feedback from my readers and realizing that something I penned made a difference for someone;
- Speaking to an audience and looking into their eyes;
- Car rides with Jim where we discover something new about one another; where we share and brainstorm and laugh (a lot);
- Connecting with a person I know I have not met before yet "knowing" them;

- Sharing the words I write with my writing partners; listening to their prose;
- Singing 'Joyful, Joyful" at the top of my lungs out on my deck, with no audience except for the cats and nature's creatures;
- A reunion with former colleagues and reminiscing about the "good old days" and all the fun and challenges we shared.

The list could go on, but I will spare you, the reader. The thing is that joy truly does exist everywhere, in the little things, in the day-to-day. Take this opportunity to sit with the questions, "Where in your life do you experience joy?" and "What makes you feel joyful?" Clear out a space in that crowdy head of yours and let the rays of joy light up the space. I guarantee that once you name the joy you have in your life, more will follow, and you will be joyful.

Travelogue

Reflective Questions

- Where in your life do you experience joy?
- What makes you feel joyful?
- Make a list. Pin it up. Look at it daily.

Create Your Joy List

In response to the previous questions, create your Joy List. Record all the things you can think of that make you feel joyful. Don't hold back. Allow yourself to be whimsical and frivolous; it is your list, after all. Find at least 12 to 15 reasons to be joyful everyday.

Key your list into the computer, print it out on beautiful parchment. Hang in a place where you can see it everyday, particularly as you begin and end the day. Read it. Remind yourself where joy resides in your life. Then, begin to watch what else shows up.

Travel Tip

The journey of life is filled with joyful moments—moments of bliss, of wonder, of happiness and contentment. They can be fleeting moments if you do not call your attention to them. On the drive through life, clear your crowdy head, make room for the experience of joy. Pay attention and place JOY in your intentions, make it your constant companion. Life will be so much more pleasant.

The Gift Certificate

The first gift of Christmas was love.
A parent's love.
Pure as the first snows of Christmas.
Richard Paul Evans, *The Christmas Box*

It came tied with a beautiful ribbon, jewel tones of ruby and amber and emerald threads woven into the fabric. The box was beautifully adorned with a tissue paper so delicate that I hesitated to touch it for fear of tearing the translucent skin. A hint of lavender tugged at my nose as I gently examined this beautiful package left for me deep inside my mother's cedar chest. Someone had taken care and pleasure in wrapping this gift for me.

I pulled at the ribbon, releasing the box from its grip. The ribbons fell gently to the side, cascading around the corners of the box. Eagerly, I scratched at the paper and then, remembering its beauty, slowed myself down. I unfolded the paper carefully so as not to tear it, preserving every special touch that had been taken as it was wrapped. As I gently peeled back the paper, the treasure held within was revealed. I reached inside and pulled from the wrapping a deep blue velvet box; you know, the type that jewelers use for something very fine and precious. I held it with reverence, feeling the texture on the palm of my hand, hesitating for a moment, anticipation rising in my chest. What could this be?

As I pulled back the lid, I closed my eyes, not wanting the moment to end. And then, opening them, I gazed with disappointment at the contents held within. The box was empty except for a single piece of paper. Tears welled up in my eyes.

I placed the box on the table in front of me and lifted the paper from its velvet nest, examining it more carefully. It was not ordinary paper but an ivory color and textured. Across the top of the paper, embossed in beautiful gold lettering, were the words Gift Certificate. This was followed by a message penned in my mother's familiar hand:

My Darling Daughter

I have wrapped this gift for you with great care for it is the legacy I leave behind and wish to offer you.

*I give to you the **Gift of Courage**—an invitation to lead your life without fear; an invitation to pursue your dreams and live the life you choose, free of the* *opinions and demands of others. It is an invitation to believe in yourself, never doubting that what you can conceive and believe, you can achieve. Lastly, it is an invitation to grab the brass ring of life and never let it go.*

*Secondly, I give you the **Gift of Love**—of love you will always have from me, even though our journey together in this lifetime has come to an end; of love for yourself—perhaps the most important gift of all; of love for others, which I encourage you to give often and freely; and of love for life and all that you touch during your time here on earth.*

*Daughter, I also give you the **Gift of Grace**—the joy of living full out, free of the burden of guilt, or blame or shame; an invitation to live your life forgiving yourself of all sins you believe you have committed against others, while also releasing the sins you believe others have committed against you. See and celebrate the abundance in your life and express gratitude for all of life's magnificence.*

*And finally, my darling daughter, I give you the **Gift of YOU**—of recognizing your own beauty, your great gifts, and perhaps most importantly, your flame, the spirit that burns deep within you. Show this light to the world—this is the **Gift of Authenticity**.*

Betty, will you do one thing for me? (And this is my last request of you.) Live this gift as I ask, and as you travel through life, give this gift freely to others. For you see, my daughter, it is in the living and the giving that the true meaning of life resides.

Love,
Mom

I placed the paper, now my most treasured possession, back in the velvet box, and gently closed the lid. Hands resting on the top of the case, I remembered my mother and the numerous other gifts she had given to me over a lifetime: patience, encouragement, a listening ear, the warmth of her arms around me, conversations over dinner, her laughter and sly sense of humor, and so much more. These, I knew, were the important gifts, more important than all the material things, the toys and clothes she had also provided. And I also knew that these were the gifts that I wanted to be remembered for, to be my legacy. What do you want yours to be?

Postscript: I wish my mother had actually written me this letter, but she did not. She did, however, leave me this gift: a desire to live boldly and courageously, a desire to love everything I touch in life, a desire to live in forgiveness and to see the abundance in my life every day, and finally, the strongest desire of all, a desire to be myself and to value the gifts I came into this world with. I thank her for this and for all the sacrifices she made for me as a single parent.

Travelogue

Reflective Question
- What GIFT do you want to give as your legacy?

Create Your Gift Certificate

Write a letter to your children, your partner or a good friend, responding to the previous question. Talk about your hopes and dreams for the others in your life and what you give to them every day as part of who you are. Write the letter in your best hand on perfumed parchment, making it as special and significant as you possibly can. When it is finished, roll it up, tie it with gold ribbon, put it in a special box, and set it aside to age like a good bottle of wine. At some point several months later, return to your gift and reread your words. Notice and savor them. When the time is right (perhaps the wedding day of a son or daughter, a significant anniversary with your spouse, a birthday for a dear friend), offer your certificate as a gift.

Travel Tip

Throughout our lives, we give and receive many gifts. Sometimes we place high value on the material ones, while diminishing the gifts of spirit and love. Pay attention to the gifts you are receiving from others—an unexpected compliment, a warm smile, the quiet presence of another and the gift of listening… the simple things that happen everyday. As we place more value on the truly important gifts, our lives become more deeply meaningful. When we give these gifts, we gently affect the lives of others and we change the world.

EPILOGUE

Travel Tips

1. Life is all about choices. You can choose to travel it in love or fear. If you choose the direction of love, you learn to acknowledge and celebrate who you are, the value you add, and the difference you make in the world. You allow yourself to make mistakes along the way and learn from them, to release the need for perfection. If you choose the direction of fear, you move forward just the same, but are plagued by self-doubt, seeing all that you are not, devaluing your own power and diminishing your importance in the world. The choice is yours—which will it be?

2. Too many YESes in your life will sidetrack you, take you down paths you did not choose for yourself. YESes can distract you from your goals, your priorities or your core values. You need to decide when NO is the **right** answer and have the courage to speak it. Like STP, NO is the additive you can put in your fuel tank that gives you added mileage, keeps your engine healthy and running smoothly, and gives you the space you need to drive the road of your own choosing.

3. You cannot see the signs crossing your path unless you stop from time to time and release yourself from your busy schedule and the long list of "to do's." Along the journey of life, you need to pull off to the side of the road occasionally and take a break. Ten minutes will do. The downtime refreshes you and allows you to stretch physically, emotionally and spiritually. You create space to take in your surroundings, to see the things which might otherwise pass you by. Don't forget to build 10-minute spirit breaks into your busy schedule. It makes the ride more pleasurable and meaningful.

4. Your bags are packed and you're ready to go, but what exactly have you packed? Just as a trunk full of baggage slows down your progress as you drive, bags laden with troubles and woes weight you down as well. What are you prepared to leave behind: the old story that no longer serves you; those who, in your view, have wronged you; life's embarrassments and foibles? It is time for each of us to lighten the load, to leave the past behind and embrace the now and the future. Once you do, you will take the brakes off your life.

5. It is often tempting, and sometimes even healthy, to travel alone. There are other times when we need the presence of others on our journey. They are there as companions, for conversation, and sometimes just to keep the seat beside you warm. There are special people among your companions who

can also be called to serve as guides. These are the friends who love and cherish your spirit and want to see you succeed. They are also the friends who hold you on course by challenging and supporting you. Remember them, seek them out and invite them to join you. They will help you when the journey seems too long, when you go in the wrong direction or when the road ahead is not clear.

6. The NEW will appear on your journey every day—new companions, new avenues to explore, new places to visit. NEW makes life exciting and the journey more interesting. It is worth pursuing. But before you decide to pursue the NEW, make sure the choices you are about to make serve your life purpose and that they are in your best interest. The NEW may simply be a distraction, challenging you to stay the course.

7. In your travels you will have many companions, yet there is only one person who will be with you every step of the way: yourself. Develop a kind and gentle relationship with this person, YOU. Love, honor and cherish yourself. Pick up your tools and build your own inner house—that sanctuary that allows you to feel safe, regardless of where you may travel. Remember, the outer houses you occupy are only temporary. Permanence is found within. Your inner house accompanies you every step of the way.

8. The belief systems you hold can serve two purposes: they can put the brakes on who you want to be and the life you want to have, or they can accelerate your journey and open you up to new possibilities. It is important to assess whether or not you have your foot on the brake or the gas pedal of your life. You can choose to discard what is not yours to carry, clear the path before you, and embrace those beliefs that nurture your soul and spirit. Then you can enjoy the ride!

9. A choice to live in fear significantly limits your experience of life, limits the choices you make as you travel, and narrows the road before you. Ask yourself, "Is this how I want to live, to journey? What would open up for me if I shifted from fear to love?" I encourage you to choose LOVE.

10. Just as your car's engine can be tuned up, so can your vocabulary. Just as you see the evidence of fine tuning in the smooth running of your car, so too will you experience this in the smooth running of your life. As you begin to harness the power of your words, and understand their role in manifesting an authentic life, the course of your life will become more focused. Begin to pay attention today to your language and use your language to give direction to your life.

11. Taking things personally can take you off course. If you allow the sting of

another's tone to hurt you, you diminish your own power. Sometimes it is appropriate to stop, even back up, asking, what am I missing here? Is this really about me? What is the context behind what I am witnessing? Put all the information you gather into a giant sieve and retain only the fine particles that make their way through. Let this feed you. Refuse to be diminished by the comments of others. Don't be derailed, and most importantly, don't take things personally.

12. Every step of the way, you are informed by the news—on radio, newspapers, magazines and television. You want to be informed. You know that living with blinders on narrows your vision, yet you must make choices. Make a choice for the positive. Feed yourself with a daily dose of inspiration. This puts more fuel in your tank and you will be guaranteed better mileage. Be firm in your intention to attract positive and inspiring SIGNS and messages to your life.

13. Let yourself "off the hook." It is time to flick your self-critic off your left shoulder and listen to a more loving inner dialogue. Give yourself the gift of forgiveness. Forgiveness is the great healer; it clears space for learning and continuing on the journey free of unnecessary baggage. Allowing yourself to forgive, learn and move on, opens you to all the possibilities the road of life has to offer you.

14. Recognize that the life you have, the journey, is already perfect. The "imperfections" you perceive are not what they seem. They are there for a reason. They are the synchronicities that inform you about your path. Trying to control them gives the illusion of keeping you on the straight and narrow, but what is really happening is that you are limiting your own learning and your ability to engage fully in your life. Releasing your need for perfection allows you to "go with the flow," to explore new roads and to enrich this experience called life.

15. Every once in a while, you need to check into the Body Shop for servicing. Your aches and pains are slowing you down, you are emotionally sluggish and underperforming. Or, you are spiritually empty, seeing no value in the way you are living your life, having lost sight of what makes you passionate or gives life meaning. STOP. Listen. Look inside your emotional and spiritual engine. What do you see? It's time for a spiritual tune-up, to evaluate what you are carrying with you and what baggage you wish to unload.

16. Pay attention. Be a sponge and soak up the wonderful events that are happening everyday, the things that you are missing or taking for granted. Seeing the extraordinary in all aspects of your life, those events or synchronicities both large and small, greases the axle, keeps the grit from slowing us down, and makes the ride rich and textured.

17. Check in with yourself from time to time to assess the status of your Plimsoll line, that point on your bow that must remain at or above the waterline so that you do not sink under the weight of life's responsibilities. Use this newly found awareness to create the work-life balance that you want to embrace. When your responsibilities and personal life are in balance, you grow increasingly aware of the meaning of your journey and where your travels are leading you.

18. The bumps in the road, those challenges that crop up on life's journey, often seem daunting or impossible. Pull off to the side of the road, and look at them from another angle. They will appear different. You will realize they are not really as big as you thought, and you will see new options and opportunities. Break the big bumps into manageable bits. You will gain a new perspective. Then get back on the road and proceed—three feet at a time.

19. Work is an expression of who you are. How you choose to show up in your workplace influences your experience as well as the experience of others. Face-to-face communication creates a bond among travelers. We are all on the same journey. Take time to meet with others, learn about their journey and speak about yours.

20. What percentage of your life does work occupy? Most of us spend 50 percent or more of our waking hours engaged in work. Recognizing this, what do you expect from work? A salary, yes, but more than that, most of us want to experience satisfaction, a sense of making a difference, community and teamwork, and a chance to express our sense of purpose. Take time to remind yourself why you work. Stay connected to your purpose through the work you do and the difference you make everyday. This keeps you connected to your higher calling and gives your life and work direction.

21. Your experience of the journey of life is an expression of how you choose to lead. It is an awareness of how you influence the world around you and the people who cross your path everyday. Choose to live large. Be generous with yourself and with others. Have an impact on every road you travel by being a positive influence. Change the world you live in by being authentically you, true to your purpose and your passion.

22. When you see the Reduce Speed sign up ahead, don't ignore it. Slow down or come to a full stop. Typically, we glide through, rarely slowing down, not really noticing the landscape around us, not really conscious of the many choices we are making. Time passes by unnoticed. Make a decision to start respecting the signs in your life. Take your foot off the gas pedal, look around and enjoy the scenery, and live your days mindfully.

23. The journey of life is filled with joyful moments—moments of bliss, of wonder, of happiness and contentment. They can be fleeting moments if you do not call your attention to them. On the drive through life, clear your crowdy head, make room for the experience of joy. Pay attention and place joy in your intentions, make it your constant companion. Life will be so much more pleasant.

24. Throughout our lives, we give and receive many gifts. Sometimes we place high value on the material ones, while diminishing the gifts of spirit and love. Pay attention to the gifts you are receiving from others—an unexpected compliment, a warm smile, the quiet presence of another and the gift of listening…the simple things that happen everyday. As we place more value on the truly important gifts, our lives become more deeply meaningful. When we give these gifts, we gently affect the lives of others and we change the world.

References

The following authors are referenced within the text of **road**SIGNS2. I thank each of them for serving as *road*SIGNS for my journey.

Arrien, Angeles. *The Four-Fold Way: Walking the Paths of the Warrior, Teacher, Healer and Visionary*. San Francisco: HarperCollins Publishers, 1993.

Bloch, Deborah P. and Richmond, Lee J. *SoulWork: Finding the Work You Love, Loving the Work You Have*. Palo Alto, California: Davies-Black Publishing, 1998.

Block, Peter. *The Answer to How Is Yes*. San Francisco: Berrett-Koehler Publishers Inc., 2002.

Bridges, William. *The Way of Transition*. Cambridge, Massachusetts: Perseus Publishing, 2001.

Cameron, Julia. *The Artist's Way: A Spiritual Path to Higher Creativity*. New York: Penguin Putnam, 1992.

Carter-Scott, Cherie. *If Life Is a Game, These Are the Rules*. New York: Broadway Books, 1998.

Cashman, Kevin. *Leadership From the Inside Out: Seven Pathways to Mastery*. Provo, Utah: Executive Excellence Publishing, 1998.

Chisholm, Tracy Lynn. "Eulogy for Julie Bedard," May 2004 (printed with permission of author)

Condrill, Jo. *Harness the Power of a Mastermind Group*. "The Toastmaster," July 2003.

Covey, Stephen. *The Seven Habits of Highly Successful People: Powerful Lessons in Personal Change*. New York: Fireside Books, Simon and Schuster, 1989.

Davis, Laura. *I Thought We'd Never Speak Again: The Road From Estrangement to Reconciliation*. New York: Harper Collins, 2002.

Dyer, Wayne. *The Power of Intention: Learning to Co-Create Your World Your Way*. Carlsbad, California: Hay House Inc., 2004.

Evans, Richard Paul. *The Christmas Box*. New York: Pocket Books, 1993.

Faith, Hope and Love: *An Inspirational Treasury of Quotations*. Philadelphia: Running Press, 1994.

Glanz, Barbara. *CARE PACKAGES for the Workplace*. New York: McGraw-Hill, 1996.

Handy, Charles. *The Hungry Spirit: Beyond Capitalism—A Quest for Purpose in the Modern World*. London: Hutchison, 1997.

Hay, Louise. *You Can Heal Your Life*. Carlsbad, California: Hay House Inc., 1984.

Jampolsky, Gerald. *Teach Only Love: The Twelve Principles of Attitudinal Healing*. Hillsboro, Oregon: Beyond Words Publishing, 2000.

Jampolsky, Gerald. *Love Is Letting Go of Fear*. Berkeley, California: Celestial Arts, 1979.

Jeffers, Susan. *Embracing Uncertainty: Breakthrough Methods for Achieving Peace of Mind When Facing the Unknown*. New York: St. Martin's Press, 2003.

Levine, Stephen. *One Year to Live: How to Live This Year As If It Were Your Last.* New York: Bell Tower, 1997.

Mills, William John. *Bring Your Work to Life: Applying the Best of You to What You Do.* Carp, Ontario: Creative Bound, 2002.

Monk-Kidd, Sue. *The Secret Life of Bees.* New York: Penguin Books, 2002.

Myss, Caroline. *Anatomy of the Spirit: The Seven Stages of Power and Healing.* New York: Three Rivers Press, 1996.

Myss, Caroline. *Why People Don't Heal and How They Can.* New York: Harmony Books, 1997.

Palmer, Parker J. *The Courage to Teach: Exploring the Inner Landscape of the Teacher's Life.* San Francisco: Jossey-Bass Publishers, 1998.

Oliver, Mary. *The Leaf and the Cloud: a poem.* Da Capo Press, Perseus Books Group, 2000.

Ruiz, Don Miguel. *The Four Agreements: A Practical Guide to Personal Freedom.* San Rafael, California: Amber-Allen Publishing, 1997.

Ruiz, Don Miguel. *The Four Agreements Companion Book.* San Rafael, California: Amber-Allen Publishing, 2000.

Schoemperlen, Diane. *Our Lady of the Lost and Found.* Toronto: Harper Perennial Canada, 2001.

Secretan, Lance. *Reclaiming Higher Ground: Creating Organizations That Inspire the Soul.* Toronto: McMillan Canada, 1996.

Secretan, Lance. *Inspire! What Great Leaders Do.* Hoboken, New Jersey: John Wiley and Sons, 2004.

Walker, Christopher. *Innerwealth: Putting the Heart and Soul Back Into Work and Life*. Oxford, United Kingdom: Capstone Publishing, 2003.

Williamson, Marianne. *A Return to Love*. New York: Harper Collins Publishers, 1993.

About the Author

Betty Healey began her career as a physiotherapist, earning her Masters degree in Educational Psychology, with a specialty in Adult Education, from McGill University in 1990. A consultant since 1997, Betty has dedicated her work to creating more inspiring and nurturing workplaces, and helping others to find purposeful and fulfilling work, develop leadership capacity and ignite team spirit.

Betty has an extensive list of clients in the private sector, particularly within the pharmaceutical industry, as well as in health care, education and public service. She has worked across Canada, the US and Scotland.

An award-winning author, Betty has also been a commentator in the media and has been interviewed in such publications as *PRIME*, *The Canadian HR Reporter*, *The Registered Practical Nursing Journal*, *Ottawa Business Journal* and *The Costco Connection*. Betty's *road*SIGNS books are based on her popular monthly e-letter of the same name, which is offered free of charge to her readers. To subscribe, contact her at betty@roadSIGNS.ca.

Betty Healey presents her audiences with a practical, hands-on approach to reconnecting with their sense of purpose in a world that is intolerant of taking time to pause.

Betty is an engaging speaker, specializing in keynote presentations to groups of all sizes. She has shifted the bar beyond motivational speaking to truly engage and inspire her audiences with topics that include *road*SIGNS *for the Journey of Life, Honor Thyself, The Gift: Courage, Authenticity, Love and Grace, Good Tired—Bad Tired*, and *You're Not the Boss of Me*.

In addition to speaking and writing, Betty facilitates both corporate and personal retreats. In all her endeavors, Betty strives to bring life into focus for her clients and audiences, encouraging them to understand the deeper purpose and meaning in their lives. Her intention is for others to experience "a life well lived."

To share Betty's message with your group or organization, please visit www.roadsigns.ca or call Creative Bound (Resources) Inc. at 1-800-287-8610.

We hope you have enjoyed *road*SIGNS2: *Travel Tips to Higher Ground*

If you would like to share your thoughts or a SIGN in your life with Betty, please feel free to e-mail betty@roadSIGNS.ca

To order additional copies of *road*SIGNS2 or any of Betty's *road*SIGNS products, please visit www.roadSIGNS.ca or call Creative Bound Inc. at 1-800-287-8610.

Organizations, businesses, retailers and book clubs—ask about our wholesale and multi-copy order discounts.

**road*SIGNS2:
Travel Tips to
Higher Ground**
ISBN 1-894439-27-9
$20.95 CAN
$17.95 US

**road*SIGNS:
Travel Tips for
Authentic Living**
ISBN 1-894439-11-2
$19.95 CAN
$15.95 US

road*SIGNS: Companion Cards
ISBN 1-894439-15-5
$19.95 CAN $15.95 US

**road*SIGNS
Companion Journal**
$14.95 CAN $11.95 US